Spiritual
Healing

Spiritual Healing

A Practical Guide
to Hands-On Healing

Jack Angelo

BARRON'S

First edition for the United States, its territories and dependencies,
and Canada published in 2002 by Barron's Educational Series, Inc.

© 2002 Godsfield Press
Text © 2002 Jack Angelo

Produced exclusively for Barron's Educational Series, Inc. by Godsfield Press.
Designed for Godsfield Press by The Bridgewater Book Company.

Illustrations by *Paul Allen*
Photography by *Mike Hemsley at Walter Gardiner Photography*

All inquiries should be addressed to:
Barron's Educational Series, Inc.
250 Wireless Boulevard
Hauppauge, NY 11788
http://www.barronseduc.com

Jack Angelo asserts the moral right to be
identified as the author of this work.

Printed and bound in China

9 8 7 6 5 4 3 2 1

ISBN 0-7641-2159-6
Library of Congress Catalog Card No. 2001094353

Bridgewater Books would like to thank the following for permission to reproduce copyright material:
CORBIS: pps. 6/7 Tony Arruza, 8 Craig Lovell, 10 Roger Ressmeyer, 15 Ralph Starkweather, 34 Digital Art, 94 Kit Kittle,
104 Steve Chen, 114 Gary Bartholemew. CORBIS/STOCKMARKET: pps. 68/69. GETTY IMAGES/STONE: pps. Anthony Marsland,
32/33 Claude Guillaumin, 39 Gandee Vasan, 110 Lonnie Duka, 128 Raymond Gehman. GETTY IMAGES/The Image Bank: pps.
42 Tom Mareschal, 52/53 Tomek Sikora, 66/67 Hans Neleman, 97 Piecework Productions, 124 Chuck Fishman.
GETTY IMAGES/Telegraph Colour Library: pps. 96 Vladimir Pcholkin, 100 Steve Bloom, 108 Elizabeth Simpson, 112 Barry Rosenthal,
130 Simon Bottomley, 135 Kevin Cruff. NOAA :p. 100. Science Photo Library: pps. 16 Francoise Sauze, 17 Garion Hutchings.

Disclaimer

This book is intended as an informational guide. The remedies, approaches, and techniques described herein are meant to complement, and not to be a substitute for, professional medical care or treatment. They should not be used to treat a serious ailment without prior consultation with a qualified health-care professional.

CONTENTS

CHAPTER 1
Where Healing Begins 6

CHAPTER 2
The Physical Body 32

CHAPTER 3
Preparing for Healing 52

CHAPTER 4
The Healing Experience 66

CHAPTER 5
Exploring Spiritual Healing 88

CHAPTER 6
Creating the Channel 120

GLOSSARY 138

INDEX 144

Where Healing Begins

When a mother reaches out to a child in distress, this is love in action. She does not have to think about it because, like all loving gestures, it comes from the heart and is unconditional and automatic. This is the basis of all healing, for the heart is the place of soul.

We are spiritual beings who have chosen to experience life in a physical universe. This means that we can choose to be so immersed in life that we can forget who we really are. Soul alerts us to this situation through a system of warning signals that may occur at the level of the body or the mind, or both. In most cases, we interpret these signals as sickness. They are the alarm call that we have lost our connection with the sacred, the source of life and love. Thus there is a direct link between our spiritual origins, our love for ourselves and each other, and our health. It is the task of spiritual healing to restore this link when it has become weakened or apparently broken.

When we reach out to help one another, the intent begins with the mind, but it is the heart that galvanizes the energy and puts it to work. When the focus is healing, the spiritual source of healing energy is tapped, and the heart and hands guide it to where it may be needed. With intention, the loving touch of comfort and reassurance gains the power to become the healing touch. Such focused energies address the cause of sickness or distress, and their effects may appear at the levels of body, emotions, or mind.

Healing is as old as humanity and its gesture appears in all forms of "hands-on" therapy. The techniques of spiritual healing can be learned, as I show in this book, but the impulse of loving service is in every person's heart. All you have to do is open your heart to awaken your natural ability to transmit energy and to create a channel for it.

Historical Perspective

The history of healing begins with the human intention to care that is common to all peoples. From this broad base it is possible to trace the development of spiritual healing.

Healing techniques acquired through centuries of experience are widespread among native peoples around the world.

At a 60,000-year-old burial site at Shanadar in northern Iraq, evidence has been found of herbs and flowers and the use of amputation. This indicates a level of care in the community—the healing of the sick and the honoring of the dead.

In 1991 the whole body of a man was found, preserved in the Alpine ice for nearly 5,000 years. The skin bore tattoos that indicated the acupuncture points that would have been used in the treatment of his two main conditions. By this means, Stone Age people could travel from place to place and still receive treatment.

The healing activities of indigenous peoples around the planet today show that ancient techniques have always been developed by individual men and women according to their personal links with the sacred. Some of these techniques combine the healing touch with the use of earth, herbs, potions and ointments, the breath, saliva, massage, manipulation, baths, and bleeding. When spirit beings are also involved, healing has a shamanistic form. Both ritual and ceremony are used to facilitate individual and group healing.

Once humans began to farm and to live in towns and cities, health care divided into two general streams—the indigenous or shamanistic form, which has continued up to the present time, and the urban healer or physician. With the development of writing, treatments could be recorded, and a new system of health care based on past knowledge and experience was born. The city states of ancient China, India, Egypt, the Middle East, Greece, and later Rome,

Medicine was already developing as a science in the Ancient World, and was well established by the Middle Ages.

all encouraged these developments, and mutual trade enabled knowledge to be shared and updated. But the religions and customs of each culture ensured the separate evolution of characteristic systems of treatment such as Ayurveda in India and the methods of Chinese Medicine.

The emblem of the Greek god of medicine, Asclepius, is a staff with two snakes (symbols of the sacred and healing) coiled around it. This is the caduceus, the emblem of medicine today. The ancient Greeks saw people as composed of spirit, mind, and body, and it was stressed that health could not be restored to the sick unless treatment addressed all these levels. Certain ways of healing were becoming the new science of medicine (Latin, *ars medicina*, "the art of healing"). These ways used the scientific method of experiment and data gathering.

Meanwhile, alongside the physician, intuitive and indigenous forms of healing still flourished according to which the ability to heal was seen not as a consequence of learning but as a natural outcome of spiritual development. Throughout the Middle East and the Hellenistic world (*c.* 400 BCE–400 CE), for example, there were hundreds of wandering teachers and mystics who exhibited various healing and psychic abilities. Among these were two famous first-century Galileans, Hanina ben Dosa and Yeshua (later known as Jesus, the Christ). Whole groups of people living an ascetic life in the desert became known for their healing prowess. One such group, the Essenes, were also referred to as the Therapeutae (from Greek, to "wait upon").

With the conversion of the Roman world to Christianity in the second century CE came profound changes in people's spirituality, which affected the development of healing. In Middle Eastern cosmology there was no division between sacred Oneness, nature, and humanity. But in the Greek and Roman world view there was a profound split. This meant that, for example, the Aramaic word used by Jesus for the One/Sacred Unity (*Alaha*) became translated as Theos, then Deus, and finally God, who has a masculine gender and is separate from human beings and the rest of creation. Since Christianity was a state religion, this world view, with its subordination of women, was enforced as a political reality. This ran counter to the early Christian practice, when the religion was still outlawed, and in which women had played a strong role, almost equal to that of men. The Church of Rome regarded this as unacceptable.

In the medieval period, the Church took control of spiritual healing, leaving medicine to trained doctors.

By the middle of the medieval period (1100–1600 CE) hands-on healing outside the Church was outlawed. A person was still considered a being of spirit, mind, and body, but the Church took over the care of the spirit, leaving the mind and body to the trained doctors of medicine. Although in Renaissance Italy there was still integration between medicine and the Church, in the rest of Europe medicine could be practiced without taking into account the spiritual life and needs of a person. This produced an inevitable split in health care from which the medical profession has still not recovered.

Europeans, in their quest for riches throughout the rest of the world, took with them notions of superiority about their religion, life values, and medicine. Where they dominated through military technology, these aspects of culture were imposed by force. The effect on health care was the spread of Western ideas about medicine and all other cultural forms were deemed inferior.

The break of science from its ancient spiritual roots allowed the development of the Newtonian mechanistic world view in the mid-seventeenth century. In the Age of Reason, life was seen as a series of machines in which the human body appeared to be a mechanical system of parts, each with basic mechanical functions. In such a system the lungs were compared to a pair of bellows, the heart to a pump, and the intestines to plumbing!

From the mid-eighteenth century, the Industrial Revolution saw further evolution and expansion of this world view, although by then medical science

needed to be able to minister to large populations. Industrialization and new economic philosophies brought demands for freedom, especially in the realm of the spirit. Many Europeans fled to North America where they felt they could start afresh.

By the middle of the nineteenth century people were demanding the freedom to practice hands-on healing without being branded as criminals. But in Britain this did not happen until the repeal of the Witchcraft Act in 1951. Healing could take place only within a church, so one way to stay within the law was to create a new Church. This came with the birth of spiritualism.

Spiritualists felt that they had recovered two important aspects of spirituality—proof of life after death (through the work of clairvoyant mediums) and the natural ability to heal. The spiritualist churches undoubtedly returned hands-on healing to the people, but a person does not have to be a spiritualist or an adherent of any religion in order to develop and practice as a healer.

With his mass rallies, the great British healer Harry Edwards played a leading role in the repeal of the Witchcraft Act, divorcing healing from this connotation. In 1955 he cofounded the National Federation of Spiritual Healers (NFSH), a nondenominational organization designed to represent healers, liaise with government and medical bodies, and present healing to the public.

Within ten years there was growing public disillusionment with medicine and by the 1970s people were turning to many types of complementary health

care, including forms of medicine practiced in other parts of the world, such as acupuncture and Ayurvedic medicine. Alongside these developments, membership of healing organizations continued to grow.

In the 1980s various bodies were offering training programs for would-be healers and those interested in personal development, including the College of Healing at Malvern, UK, and the College of Psychic Studies in London. The NFSH has an extensive training program and is now the world's leading healing organization, with a network of centers around the world. Healing is also widely practiced in spiritualist churches while its presence in the established Church has declined over the centuries.

With these developments in complementary health care has come the recognition of indigenous and shamanistic forms and a fresh understanding of the role of personal development and spirituality in human and planetary health.

"Healing could take place only within a church, so a way to stay within the law was to create a new Church. This came with the birth of spiritualism."

Since the turn of the twentieth century, science has presented us with new dilemmas about the meaning of life, though many see scientific discoveries, especially in genetics and quantum physics, pointing to eternal spiritual truths. The role of spiritual healing in the twenty-first century is to help people to reconnect with these truths and to recover a sense of the sacred in every aspect of life.

Subtle-Energy Medicine and the Holistic View of Health

The energies of healing travel at speeds faster than the speed of light. These are known as subtle energies. Subtle-energy medicine embraces all therapies that make use of these energies to help a client. Spiritual healing emphasizes that the source of all energy is spiritual, so this is its approach to subtle-energy healing. We are first and foremost spiritual beings living in a spiritual universe. This accounts for spiritual healing's particular holistic vision. For some, holism may be looking at the whole body, not just the part that has the symptoms of a condition. Others go further, also taking into consideration mental and emotional states.

We live on a planet that behaves like a living organism, and we share a range of planetary environments with the animals and plants of the earth family. Modern ecologists consider that humans are part of a complicated ecosystem in which all parts are interdependent and of equal value. The shamanistic view of life is that all things are of equal value because they are one within sacred Oneness. Spiritual healing aligns itself with this view, according to which we are one not only with the total universe but with all levels of being, including the subtle levels that occur outside the physical and the space/time framework. It is this underlying fact of oneness at all levels that makes spiritual healing possible. Because spiritual healing is the only therapeutic system that honors, celebrates, and works with all levels of being, its holistic vision is unique within health care.

*Each human being on the planet
is part of a sacred Oneness, and so our
individual well-being is closely
linked with that of everyone else.*

The Network of Consciousness

All energy, and therefore all matter, emanates from the one source of consciousness, the source of unconditional love. This means that all energy is conscious to some degree, creating a network of consciousness in which all forms of energy are linked energetically. The implications for our own and the planet's health are far-reaching and account for many of the spiritual laws of life such as the interconnection of all things, so whatever affects one life form or energy pattern affects all others.

The spiritual laws of life are the outward manifestations of Oneness and are laws about the behavior of energy, providing a real basis for morality. The law of cause and effect, for example, means that every action will produce a reaction. Oneness also means that if I hurt another I hurt myself. "Do unto others what you would have them do unto you" is therefore an understanding of energetic reality. Our mind enables us to choose whether to heed or disregard how energy behaves. Mind has the capacity for memory, so we can recall our life experiences and use them to enhance our life in the present.

In considering our own health it is helpful to realize that what we think and the way we think are registered by the cells of the body, through the network of consciousness. Medical practitioners as well as psychologists have long realized that we can think ourselves into illness. Our ability to do this equally means that we can think ourselves out of illness if only we know how to.

The experience of spiritual healing is that illness is very often our soul's way of alerting us that we have become disconnected from our sacred reality. The language of soul is via feelings. We feel what is right or wrong for us. When we ignore our feelings, especially the intuitive ones, the network of consciousness allows the energy to impact on our body. We begin to feel with the body consciousness. This often means that something hurts. Our body is our friend, telling us when things are not as they should be, even when the truth hurts. And like a true friend its love for us is unconditional—it is there for us no matter what we do. But when something hurts, our friendship with our body is put to the test.

The Soul Journey

When pain draws our attention to the body we may wonder where feelings and mind fit into the picture. The holistic vision of spiritual healing is that the mind, emotions, and body are instruments of soul. Each has a part to play in the heroic journey that every person undertakes—the soul journey.

Our spiritual home is a place of absolutes, a place of total love. In the spiritual realm we cannot know what this means because there is nothing to compare it with. We would have to be able to experience the absence of love as well as its totality. We can do this on the earth plane because it is a place of duality, where all opposites are present—

light and dark, hot and cold, pain and pleasure, separation as well as oneness.

In energetic terms, the transition from the energy of soul to the relatively dense and slow-moving energy of the body and physical life is immense. For such a special trip we need a series of energy patterns through which all levels of energy may be experienced and processed. A bridging level between the energy of soul and the body is provided by what is known as the etheric body. Vibrating faster than the physical, the etheric body may be sensed as projecting from 1–4 inches (3–10 cm) beyond the physical body. It is quite natural, and also necessary, for us to sense subtle energies. Perceived sensations are then conveyed to the brain for interpretation; some of us may see subtle-energy patterns while others may feel, hear, smell, or even taste them. The ability to interpret them visually is known as clairvoyance.

Our natural ability to sense subtle energetic material outside ourselves is a form of psychic awareness, while the ability to sense this material within (such as a soul message) is known as intuitive awareness. The etheric body facilitates the passage of information both to and from the body. In order to be conscious of our experiences we have a mind. This generates thoughts and gives us the power to choose our way of being and how we think. Feelings are communicated to our body consciousness via

*Take time to work out
your soul journey and think about
where you are going in your life.*

the etheric body. When thoughts and feelings impact on the physical body they produce emotions. So we experience a physical life, an emotional life, and a mental life. But who is this "we?"

Perhaps the most heroic aspect of soul's experience is that it has to operate through a personality. This is a direct effect of the network of consciousness. Matter has consciousness; therefore, each cell of the body has consciousness. From the moment that we begin to develop in our mother's womb, our body is accumulating conscious experience that is stored in the mind. As our genetic makeup and our life experience interact, a conscious being emerges known as the personality or ego. It is through this conscious being, our personality, that our soul will have to express itself and experience life.

The soul is our reality, but, for many, the person that we are aware of seems to be the only real part of us. On this earth walk we are both soul and the personality, and spiritual healing works with all aspects and levels of a person.

*"The soul is our reality, but, for many, the person that we are aware
of seems to be the only real part of us."*

The Human Energy Field (Aura)

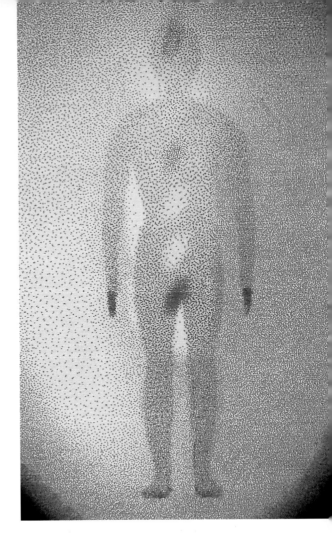

All the energetic levels of a person (spiritual, mental, emotional, etheric, physical) are vibrating at different speeds. The faster the speed of the energy, the greater distance it will travel. Perception of this area of energy around a person has been known throughout history as the aura (from Greek *avra*, "breeze," because, like the wind, the aura can be felt but not seen with everyday vision). But when we relax and allow our psychic sense to operate, we may detect the aura quite easily. Usually we "see" it because our brain interprets the energy field as something it sees.

"The physical body radiates a certain amount of energy, especially in the form of heat."

Spiritually developed people radiate a great deal of light, especially around the head, which has been depicted by artists as a halo.

The energy field can be sensed as a series of layers of energy with each layer vibrating at faster and faster speeds as the energy moves out from the body. The physical body radiates a certain amount of energy, especially in the form of heat. Next can be seen the etheric body, which is vibrating a little faster than the physical. In the energy zone around the etheric we process emotional material, and beyond this is the zone where we process mental material. Because these zones may be detected as distinct layers of energy, they are often referred to as "bodies" but this is where their

likeness to a body ends. Surrounding these detectable zones is the energy of soul.

Soul energy appears to disperse into separate human beings, but with sufficient sensitivity it will be realized that in fact there is no "edge" to an individual soul and that each soul merges with every other. In reality, there is only one soul. Each person, with their components of physical body, etheric body, and mind, is contained, as it were, within soul (spirit).

Long ago, Australian Aborigines and Native Americans experienced this fact and expressed it as "Oneness." When the Lakota Native Americans perform any sacred act, for example, they use the phrase *mitakuye oyasin*, "all my relations," or "we are all related." This is also true in the Middle East where Hebrew, Aramaic, and Arabic words meaning The One and Oneness have been misleadingly translated into European languages as the personal form "God." Spiritual healing acknowledges this law of Oneness. Healing energy, like love, is a constant energetic presence that we simply need to be open to and to use.

The aura is a record of what is happening to us moment by moment. At each level, whatever we are processing is detectable within the levels of the aura. We are all aware of each other's aura, which explains why we often take an instant like or dislike to somebody—we are affected by that person's energy field. We can often pick up a person's feelings or thoughts because we are unconsciously interacting with his or her aura.

Clairvoyant or psychic vision is the ability to "see" the aura of others. It may appear as areas of colored light around a person, and these colors may change as their mood or pattern of thinking changes. When people are depressed we say they "have the blues." This dark blue or gray color is the color of unhappiness in the aura. When we "see red" (get angry) we may be seeing with our inner sight the

energy of aggression welling up from our basal energy center. When a person is "green with envy" an unpleasant acidic green light may appear to emanate from the body. If we are "in the pink" we may not just be feeling healthy but actually glowing happily within an aura of pink light.

This natural ability, which is well developed in animals, is something we can all develop. The first step is to accept the possibility and then to relax our everyday senses and allow the psychic sense to operate without interference. Let's look at some ways to open up our own sensitivity.

Auras can have different colors depending on the emotions being experienced by the individuals concerned.

Exercise 1:
Sensing Energy with the Hands

1 Make yourself comfortable. Hold your hands with the palms facing up, about body-width apart. Allow them to relax. Let your mind gently focus on your palms. What do you sense? Keep your focus and see if your sensations begin to change.

2 Now close your hands slowly so that your fingers press into your palms. Do this a number of times until your palms begin to feel energized.

3 Hold your hands palms-up again. Allow your hands to sense as before. With the hands energized do you notice or feel any difference?

4 You are surrounded by a universal energy field. Your intention is to feel this energy as it is drawn toward your hands. What do you sense now? Allow yourself to be open to any new sensation.

5 Finally, your intention now is to send energy to someone who needs your help. Allow a picture or name of a person to drift into your mind. The first to appear is the one to send out to. Let your intention rest in the palms of your hands. Do not try to manipulate the energy, simply be aware of what happens. Allow your hands to sense without imposing any conditions on what you think should be happening.

Keep a note of all your exercise work.
Accept yourself and your sensations.
This is the first step in building your
personal database.

Exercise 2:
Sensing the Aura with a Partner

you sense the "edge" of his energy field. Stop moving toward your partner at this point. The sensation is a little like bouncing or pushing gently against a very soft resistance. This "resistance" is the place in your partner's field where you are able to sense the energy. Notice how far your hands are from his body. When you compare this place to the diagram of the aura, estimate what part of your partner's field you are able to sense. Do you pick up any other impressions?

3 Allow your hands to move again, slowly and gently, into your partner's energy field. Make a mental note of your impressions. Finish the palm-sensing when you are about 2–3 inches (5–8 cm) from your partner's body.

4 Compare the information from your palm-sensing with your earlier impressions. Share your total impressions with your partner. Now change roles so that you are the subject of the exercise this time.

1 Ask your partner to stand or sit comfortably. Stand or sit a few yards away from him. Take a few slow breaths and relax your body. Close your eyes and allow your focus to drift gently toward your partner. Allow any impressions you receive to appear and then disappear. Make a mental note of them, whatever they are.

2 Now raise your hands in front of you, about shoulder high, with the palms facing your partner. Move slowly toward your partner until

5 Add this work to your database. Remember that it describes how sensitive you are at this point, but it will be very useful to look back on at a later date.

The Etheric Body

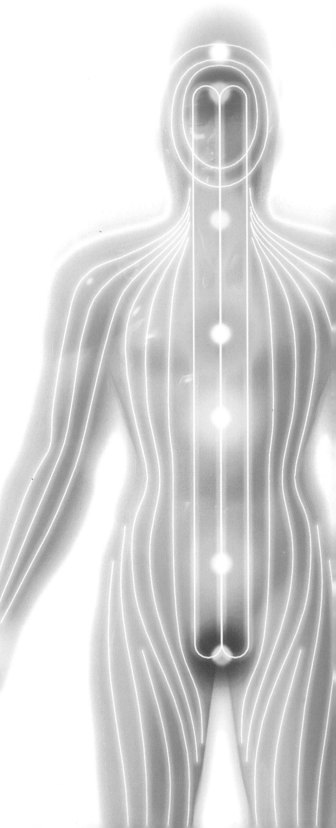

In the two previous exercises you were becoming more aware with your physical senses, but also with your psychic senses. They are your personal discoveries and need not be compared with anyone else's. Psychic awareness, in particular, tends to be a very individual thing, for each of us has an individual way of interpreting what is sensed or perceived. Furthermore, perception changes as it is developed. Be confident and relaxed in all your spiritual-healing work. You are making yourself available to a special energy that is always around you, ready to be used, and you are doing this in your own individual way. The key to being available is your own heartfelt intention.

All your sensations are transmitted to all levels of your being via your etheric body. The word "etheric" comes from Greek, meaning the upper regions of heaven. This is because ancient Greek seers noticed that the etheric body appeared to rise out of the physical at the time of death. As discussed earlier this etheric energy pattern or body acts as a bridge between the vibrations of the subtle energies of spirit, mind, and emotion and the relatively much slower energies of the physical body. In this way it also acts as a bridging place for soul as it enters the body and when it leaves at the time of passing over (death).

Here, in the etheric body, is the blueprint or template for the physical; therefore, the layout of the physical body reflects the layout of the etheric body. The etheric body appears in clairvoyant vision as having the shape of the physical body although composed of a finer material, with a smoky or light bluish color. Running throughout this body are many hundreds of fine lines or channels of light, so the etheric body seems to be lit up from within.

Where the lines of light cross each other, light vortexes occur in varying sizes. These light vortexes, acting as centers of energy, have come to be known as *chakras*, from the Sanskrit *chakram*, a wheel. Indian seers gave these vortexes this simple name because they appeared to be whirling areas of light

The etheric body contains a number of light-emitting channels and vortexes, known as chakras.

that looked like a moving cartwheel. This system of subtle-energy channels and centers is the basis for the meridians and energy points used in the practice of acupuncture.

Clairvoyant vision confirms that all living creatures, whether animal or plant, originate from an etheric "body." Planet earth too has an etheric base structure, giving rise to the idea that the planet has its own system of chakras or energy centers. The lines of power known as ley lines, which can be detected by dowsers and psychic sensitives, seem to be evidence of an etheric grid of energy channels that may have similar functions to those of the energy meridians of the human body.

For us, the etheric body is constructed so that it can transmit subtle energies to the physical level, via the mental and emotional zones of the energy field. It also conducts mental and emotional energies to the physical, using the same energetic structures. Transmission is two-way; therefore, all energies, including the physical, can be conducted to levels where energy is vibrating at a relatively faster rate. The etheric structures that allow for the two-way transmission of subtle energies are the system of interconnected chakras.

The functions of the etheric body, outlined above, make it the central area of study for spiritual healers, because through this body, via the chakra system, all healing energies must travel. Whatever techniques a healer may use, the focus of the work will always be consciously or unconsciously on the chakra system.

The Chakras

With sensitive awareness, the chakras appear as concentrated areas of light. The larger chakras tend to be conical or bell-like structures with a connection to one of the many channels running throughout the etheric body. The bell-like shape gathers and distributes energies. Patterning on the inside of the "bell" causes the energies to vibrate to certain colors, which tend to change as different energetic transactions are taking place.

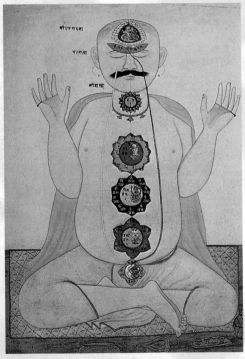

The system of chakras forms a link between our physical bodies and other levels of being.

There are many hundreds of light centers in the etheric body located in positions related to particular organs of the physical body. One of the most important functions of the network is to convey the life force (known as *qi* in Chinese and *prana* in Sanskrit) to the nucleus of every cell in the physical body. Each chakra facilitates the flow of subtle energies to and from the physical body and the other levels of being. They can also absorb as well as emanate subtle energies. This means that what we think and feel may be energetically conveyed to the physical body, and what happens to the body is conveyed to the other levels. Furthermore, impulses from soul are sent to us via the chakra system. We may not be consciously aware of these transactions, but they are still occurring at every instant of our life.

The Seven Major Chakras

The seven larger chakras, aligned with the spine, are situated along a central channel in the etheric body. Their size (1–4 inches/3–10 cm across) is related to their function and varies from person to person. Each chakra processes energies associated with specific life issues related to our soul journey. These energies, when in a state of harmony with each other, vibrate with the same frequencies as the colors that are effectively the human rainbow within—red, orange, yellow, green, blue, indigo, violet. The energies impact on the physical body via the endocrine glands and from there may move out to affect the surrounding organs.

The Chakras and their Related Life Issues

Chakra	Vibratory Color	Related Life Issues
Crown	Violet/purple	Spirituality; the incoming Light
Brow	Indigo/royal blue	Intuitive and psychic awareness; soul knowledge
Throat	Sky blue	Communication; expression; trust
Heart	Green	Unconditional love; harmony; care of others
Solar plexus	Golden yellow	Mind; personal power; sense of self
Sacral	Orange	Creativity; sexuality; joy
Base	Red	Body; nature; planet; sensuality; survival

The Base Chakra

The Base Chakra

Located at the base of the spine, this center is our link with the physical world. It absorbs energy from the planet and is able to "refine" this energy for use within our system.

The base chakra processes all issues related to our survival and feelings of security: our body, the planet, and the natural world. Its energies impact on the body via the adrenal glands. These deal with our ability to defend ourselves, either by standing our ground or leaving a situation. Stress threatens our survival and so activates the adrenal glands. Base center energies can also affect the pelvis, hips, legs, and feet.

When in a state of balance, the base chakra vibrates to the color red.

The Sacral Chakra

The Sacral Chakra

Opposite the sacral bones of the spine, below the navel, this center processes all issues connected with our creativity, sexuality, ability to play and express joy.

The energies of the sacral chakra impact on the body via the sex glands. They may also affect the urogenital organs, the uterus, kidneys, the lower digestive organs, and lower back.

When in a state of balance, the sacral chakra vibrates to the color orange. It also absorbs vitality energy from the cosmos.

The Solar Plexus Chakra

The Solar Plexus Chakra

Named after the large nerve plexus, it is located just below the diaphragm and above the navel. This energy center processes all issues connected with the mind and emotions: personal power and sense of self. The most powerful emotion we generate is fear, the opposite of love, which we feel in this chakra. Feelings of discomfort in this region may affect the diaphragm and our ability to breathe properly.

The energies of this center impact on the body via the islets of Langerhans in the pancreas. They may also affect the gastric nerve plexuses, the digestive system, pancreas, liver, gall bladder, and stomach.

When in a state of balance, the solar plexus chakra vibrates to the color golden yellow. It also absorbs vitality energy from the cosmos.

The Heart Chakra

Located in the center of the chest, this chakra processes all issues concerned with love, especially unconditional love, and concern for others. Here we are aware of the messages of soul. At this level, feelings are unconditional, but once they are allowed to interact with our conditioned mind (in the solar plexus center) we may not heed their message.

The Heart Chakra

The energies of the heart center impact on the body via the thymus gland and can further affect the heart, lungs, chest, upper back, and arms.

When in a state of balance, the heart chakra vibrates to the color emerald green. Green is the color of balance, and this reflects another function of this chakra, which is to balance energies moving up the system with those moving down the system.

The Throat Chakra

The Throat Chakra

This chakra processes all issues of communication and expression. Everything we create is expressed through the throat. This chakra also deals with all issues of truth, trust, and the true expression of who we really are and whether we are able to be authentic.

Throat chakra energies impact on the body via the thyroid gland. They may also affect the pharyngeal nerve plexus, the neck, the organs of the throat, the ears, nose, mouth, and teeth.

When in a state of balance, the throat chakra vibrates to the color sky blue.

The Brow Chakra

Located in the middle of the forehead, this center processes all issues of psychic and intuitive awareness.

The Brow Chakra

It receives soul knowledge before it reaches the brain so that we are able to balance the power of mind and mental reasoning. Known since ancient times as the Third Eye (because it processes subtle forms of perception), this center presents us with the challenge of listening to and trusting our intuition and psychic awareness as life skills.

Its energies impact on the body via the pituitary gland and hypothalamus of the brain. Just as these organs monitor and stimulate all the other glands, so the brow chakra oversees and monitors the energetic activities of all the other chakras. Brow center energies may also affect the nervous system, the brain, face, and eyes.

When in a state of balance, the brow chakra vibrates to the color indigo or royal blue.

The Crown Chakra   *The Crown Chakra*

Our direct link with the Source and the gateway for spiritual light, the crown chakra processes all issues arising from our relationship with Oneness. Its energies impact on the body via the pineal gland in the brain, and affect the brain and the rest of the body.

When in a state of balance, the crown chakra vibrates to the color violet or purple.

Sensing the Seven Major Chakras

The awareness you used in sensing the human energy field becomes more focused now to locate the chakras. If necessary activate your palms again as in Exercise 1, "Sensing Energy with the Hands" (page 18).

Exercise 3:
Locating the Major Chakras with a Supine Person

1 Have your partner lie comfortably on the floor or on a healing couch. Make sure the legs and arms are uncrossed. Ask your partner to relax and breathe normally. Hold your palms about 2 feet (60 cm) away from your partner's crown, in line with the spine. Check that you are relaxed and breathing normally too. Note any sensations. Is energy leaving your palms or being absorbed into them?

2 Now slowly move your palms toward your partner's crown chakra. Recall the bouncy feeling of energetic resistance that you felt when sensing the aura. When you are aware of a similar sensation emanating from your partner's crown chakra keep your hands in this place and note where they are. You have located the crown chakra. Note any sensations.

3 Slowly and gently bring your palms down over your partner's head until they are opposite the brow center, the same initial distance away as before. Gently move your palms toward the brow center until you sense its energies. Stop the movement of your hands once you have located the brow chakra. Note any sensations.

4 Again, with slow and gentle movements, move your palms again until they are positioned above the throat chakra and then move toward the center until you locate its energies. Note any sensations.

5 One by one, move on to the heart, solar plexus, sacral, and base chakras, starting well away from the chakra and moving toward it, stopping your hand movements once you have located the energies.

6 Change roles now so that you can experience your partner's hands moving near your energy centers.

Exercise 4:
Locating the Chakras with a Seated Person

The energies of a chakra may also be detected at the back of the body as well as the front. Sometimes clients are not able to lie on the healing couch and need to be treated in a chair. This exercise will ensure that you can work with a person in this position.

1 For the purpose of this exercise make sure that your partner is relaxed and seated sideways on a chair or on a stool so that the back is not covered. The feet should be flat on the floor and uncrossed. The hands should not be joined or crossed. Stand at your partner's free side, relax, and breathe normally.

2 Raise your hands with the palms tilted in to face the top of your partner's head. Again, this should be some 2 feet (60 cm) above the crown chakra. Slowly allow both hands to move down toward the crown chakra until your palms are aware of its energies. Stop and note the position of your hands. Remember, you are sensing with both palms. How far away from the chakra are they? What sensations are you aware of?

3 Now move your hands down until the palms are opposite your partner's brow chakra, with one palm in front and the other behind the head. Slowly bring them in toward the chakra, as if it is a sphere of energy you can sense at both sides of your partner's head. Again, stop when you sense the energies of the brow center with each palm.

4 Move on to locate the throat, heart, solar plexus, and sacral chakras, sensing the energies with your palms at the front and back of the body. All your movements should be slow, deliberate, and gentle. At some point you may need to draw up another chair to sit on, or you could kneel on the ground, whichever is most comfortable for you.

5 Because of the curvature of the spine when a person is seated, the base chakra is sensed with the two palms making an angle of about 45 degrees, not horizontally as for the sacral chakra. The palm at the front of the body should be held above the groin while the palm at the back is held below the base of your partner's spine.

6 Change roles, and once you have finished, share your experiences.

The Chakras of the Hands and Feet

A study of the main chakras used in healing includes those in the palms of the hands and soles of the feet (making 11). Like all chakras they absorb as well as transmit energies.

The Palm Chakras

You have already been using your palm chakras in all the previous exercises. In most cases you have been absorbing energy with them, and your brow center has conveyed the information to your brain to be interpreted. But in the second part of Exercise 1, "Sensing Energy with the Hands" (page 18), your intention was to allow your palm chakras to transmit energy to help someone. In this way you became aware of the different sensations of both giving and receiving subtle energies.

It is important also to recall that the palm chakras are linked energetically to the heart chakra. This is the powerful link of love that is so important in healing. The heart center is involved in opening us to the healing energy of the Source, conveying it to the hands if this is the way we are carrying out the work.

The Sole of the Foot Chakras

These chakras absorb energies from the planet. They also allow us to ground or "earth" energies, a process that is essential when we need to be in touch with our physical body. This is important in healing where

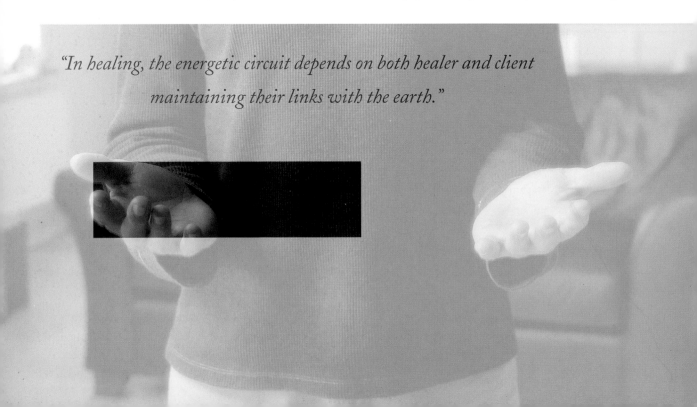

"In healing, the energetic circuit depends on both healer and client maintaining their links with the earth."

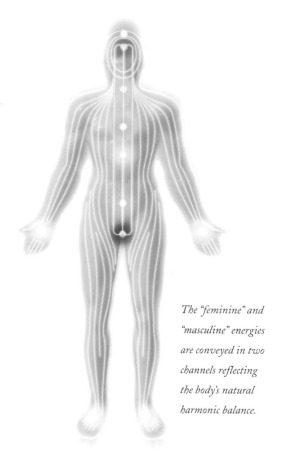

The "feminine" and "masculine" energies are conveyed in two channels reflecting the body's natural harmonic balance.

the energetic circuit depends on both healer and client maintaining their links with the earth.

The chakras in the soles of the feet are linked energetically to the base chakra. This aids the grounding process and also allows earth energies to enter the etheric body to be conducted up the central channel.

The Role of the Chakras in Energetic Balance

As shown in the illustration above (right), two channels on each side of the central channel are connected to the base and brow chakras. These channels convey two complementary energies that have come to be termed feminine and masculine. Both energy streams are present in all persons, whatever their gender. They reflect the dual nature of life in the physical universe with its series of

opposites. One of the keys to human health is the harmony of the polarity of the two streams (as illustrated above). This polarity is also reflected in the almost total symmetry of the body—a symmetry it has derived from the etheric body. Thus the hands and feet are also linked energetically to body polarity. In most cases this is checked during any healing session by looking at the state of polarity balance revealed by the chakras in the sole of the foot. But this check can also be carried out at the shoulders when you are intuitively impressed to do so. Thus, we are able to assess the energetic polarity balance of a person via both the chakras of the palms and the soles of the feet.

The next exercise examines the polarity balance in your partner's subtle-energy system by working with the feet.

Exercise 5:
Checking Polarity Balance

1 Have your partner lie comfortably on the floor or on the healing couch. Position yourself opposite her feet. Relax and breathe normally. Allow your gaze to scan your partner's body without focusing on any part. Do you receive any impressions?

2 Now raise your palms until they are opposite your partner's feet and some 6–12 inches (15–30 cm) away from them. Focus your mind on your palms to locate the chakras in your partner's soles. You may need to move your palms a little in order to locate the chakras. If energy leaves your palm centers, your partner needs this energy to bring balance. Notice if one or both feet behave in this way.

3 Discuss your sensations with your partner. Do they relate to how your partner was feeling and has there been any change?

4 Change roles and again discuss your sensations together.

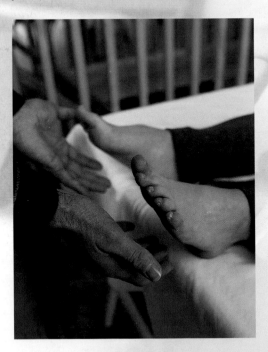

At a later date practice working with the shoulders in the same way. Hold your palms opposite your partner's shoulder joints about 6–12 inches (15–30 cm) from them. Discuss your sensations with your partner. You now have experience in working with the 11 chakras that play a crucial role in the life of a person and in the healing routine. We mentioned earlier how the seven major chakras vibrate to the same colors as the rainbow. Here is an exercise where you can see for yourself the colors of the energies you are processing at any given time.

Exercise 6:
Sensing Color in
the Major Chakras

For this exercise your partner should have worked with Exercise 4, "Locating the Chakras with a Seated Person" (page 27). You will gain the most benefit from the exercise if you can accept your inner vision and not expect the relevant color of the balanced state to appear.

1 Sit comfortably on a chair with your feet flat on the floor. Your hands should be unjoined and resting palms-down on your thighs. (The palms-down position allows a person to be more aware of internal processes.) Relax and breathe normally. Close your eyes and focus your attention on your crown chakra.

2 Your partner is there to aid your focus and expression and should stand at one side of you in order to hold one palm comfortably near the back of your neck, opposite your throat chakra, having located its energies. Your partner should raise their other arm so that the palm locates your crown chakra energies. As you look at your internal "screen," what color, if any, do you see? Do you see anything else such as patterns or symbols? Simply accept what comes. Share your sensations with your partner.

3 Your partner now asks you to focus on the brow chakra, keeping the same palm

opposite your throat chakra, at the back of your neck, while moving the other palm to come opposite your brow. Again, describe what you experience.

4 Move from the brow to the throat, heart, solar plexus, sacral, and base chakra in the same way. Each time describe your sensations to your partner.

5 Having reached the base chakra, your partner can move the hands away and you can open your eyes. Allow your partner to check out your experience of each chakra. When ready, change roles and share experiences. Remember, this is not a healing exercise. You are simply helping each other to sense color in the chakras. If you have a completely balanced set of colors—violet, indigo, blue, green, yellow, orange, red—you probably need to do the exercise again since it is highly unlikely for any person to be in this ideal state.

The Physical Body

When we think of the soul journey that all of us have decided to undertake, the physical body could certainly be described as a temple for soul since each person's body is a sacred vehicle with a sacred purpose—to experience physical life. Every aspect of us is grounded in our bodies. Our spirituality (experience of the sacred) takes place in our bodies, not somewhere else. The body needs to be celebrated, honored, respected, and cared for.

But it would also be helpful for us to remember that soul is there for us as a place of sanctuary, too. We need to find ways to retire to this sanctuary on a regular basis, fully grounded in the body, to remember who we really are. For we are not the body.

Most of the time we feel most in touch with the body. When something goes wrong with it we look for help. This malfunction of the body is what your client will bring to you. This is the part of us that carries a strong message that something is out of harmony or that we are suffering the consequences of our disconnection from the sacred.

In order to honor and respect the body, we need to get to know it as well as possible. Our study of spiritual healing will include an explanation of the subtle as well as the physical aspects and functions of the body and its systems. This understanding should help us to be more aware that we are responsible for our own health and that health-care professionals are there to help us to become whole again. The body has an innate ability to heal itself. It simply requires the right conditions for this to happen. Spiritual healing affirms that these conditions originate at a spiritual level and that the body needs the support of the spirit.

The Systems
of the Body

Through the influence of soul's needs, the etheric cooperates with our genetic makeup to create the systems of the physical body. The facilitator is the network of consciousness. This finds concentrated expression in the nucleus of every cell, the fundamental unit of biological life. The genetic code (DNA) that we bring with us, which is a combination of our parents' genetic makeup, helps

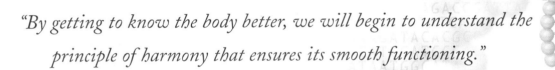

"By getting to know the body better, we will begin to understand the principle of harmony that ensures its smooth functioning."

to differentiate the cells in the early days of our development as an embryo. The genes then influence the cells to combine to form the body's organs and tissues. Next, the organs go on to form definite life systems. The activities of each cell are directed by the nucleus, which in turn is energized by the life force, a subtle energy without which life would cease.

Everything that happens in the body is a result of the same coordination and cooperation that brought about the formation of the body's systems. In a healthy body, each organ and each system acts for the benefit of the whole. A feature of many diseases, such as cancer, is the breakdown of this coordinated activity. When this happens, the body is sounding an alarm.

By getting to know the body better, we will begin to understand the principle of harmony that ensures its smooth functioning. When we consider our fitness, our diet, or an illness, we tend to think only of those parts of the body concerned. We should try to

educate ourselves to think holistically so that we always see the body as a balanced whole. Each system has a relationship with all the others. Within any system, each organ or tissue has a relationship, and within these, each cell has a relationship. Through these energetic relationships, every part of the body is aware of what is happening to the whole.

An account of body relationships is conveyed to the etheric via the relevant glands and chakras. They are then available to the mind and soul. This means equally that the mind can influence the activities of the body, and so can feelings. Thus balance and harmony between the levels of our being are the key to health, which could be described as the continuous coordinated functioning of the cells.

In the following exercise we will reintroduce ourselves to the body and see if we gain any insight from this procedure.

Exercise 7:
Friendship with the Body

1 Lie or sit comfortably. Take a few conscious breaths and relax the body. Close your eyes and listen to your breathing. Without straining, focus entirely on the sound of your breathing.

2 Now notice how your belly moves to facilitate the breathing. Its surface is moving to a gentle rhythm. This surface is your skin. Slowly scan the surface of your skin, all over your body. This may take you inside your mouth, your ears, and other orifices.

3 Your tour of the skin will eventually take you into various other systems of your body. Take your time. Allow your body to guide you.

4 Realize that your skin covers muscles that are giving definition to your body. Take time to acquaint yourself with as many muscles as you can. You do not need to know their names to know what they do.

5 Supporting all these other structures is the skeleton. Take a trip round your bones. Perhaps there are more than you realized.

6 See if your tours help you to find out what makes it all work. What seems to be happening without your even knowing about it or giving any commands? You have been breathing throughout all your tours. Gently and surely, the rhythm of life has been coursing through you. Thank your body and promise yourself some more quality time with it.

The Skeleton

There are 206 separate bones that make up the framework of the adult body, each one a masterpiece of natural engineering. The bony skeleton weighs about 20 pounds (9 kilos) yet it may hold up a mass of muscles and organs that weigh about five times more. The structure of the larger bones, such as the thigh, makes them stronger, pound for pound, than reinforced concrete. The whole skeleton is held together at the joints by tough ligaments and tendons and is moved by sets of paired muscles.

"The skeleton does more than provide a chassis for the body vehicle, allowing us to stand upright and to move around."

In a two-month-old fetus the skeleton of flexible cartilage may be detected. Just before and just after birth more calcium is added to the cartilage in the process called ossification, which continues until we are between 18 and 20. By then, the bones contain 99 per cent of all our stored calcium.

The skeleton does more than provide a chassis for the body vehicle, allowing us to stand upright and to move around. The skull and vertebrae enclose the brain and spinal nerve cord, and the ribcage protects the heart and lungs. Marrow inside certain bones produces red blood cells, which carry oxygen and nutrients, while in others it produces white blood cells, which are a vital part of our immune system. The inner compact material of a bone provides its great strength and surrounds the marrow. Each layer interacts with the others through a system of nerves and blood vessels.

At a subtle level, the bones provide a memory base of every incident that may happen to the skeleton. Evidence of this may be seen when the healer is scanning a client's skeleton and finds a place calling for energy. The client may be surprised because an injury to that part happened several years before. The bones are linked at this level by an energy circuit that follows the basic outline of the skeleton (see illustration opposite).

Smaller chakras are present at every joint, the energy centers of the skeletal circuit. As we shall see, this circuit is scanned by the healer during the first part of the healing session. Like the chakras, the skeletal energy circuit needs to be in a state of balance and this can be checked through the feet, as in Exercise 5, "Checking Polarity Balance" (see page 30). In this case the hands are held closer to the feet with the intention of assessing skeletal balance.

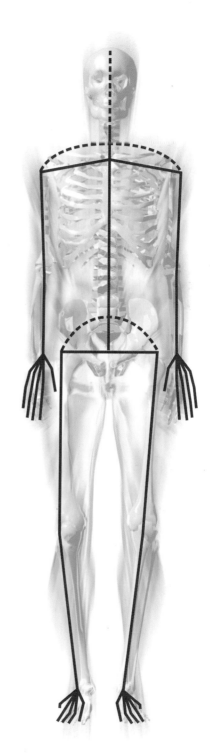

The skeleton has a main energy circuit and energy centers at every joint, which all need to be in balance.

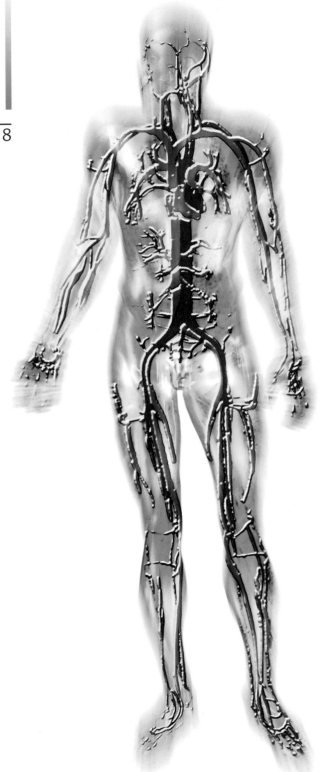

The Circulatory System

The life-sustaining materials that all the organs of the various systems need are carried in the bloodstream. The blood also carries the waste products produced by the body to those organs that will process them for elimination, for example the kidneys, which deal with the excretion of toxins and urine.

The major part of the circulatory system is made up of arteries carrying 15 percent of our blood supply, which is oxygenated. Veins carry about 70 percent of the blood, which is depleted of oxygen and laden with waste products.

The circulation of blood throughout these vessels is ensured by the action of the heart. This muscular organ lies in the center of the chest with its apex a little to the left of center. The heart acts like two pumps in one, each with two chambers. The right side receives blood from all areas of the body, which is partly depleted of oxygen, and pumps it to the lungs. The left side of the heart receives the oxygenated blood from the lungs and pumps it to the rest of the body. Valves in the heart prevent the two kinds of blood from mixing. The pulse you can feel in your wrist, or at a major artery such as in the neck, is the pressure wave that moves through the arterial system as the heart pumps blood into it.

At a subtle level, the body has four support systems. These are the etheric, the nervous, the endocrine, and the vascular (blood). The subtle energies of the first three are transported by the blood to every cell in the body. One of the important

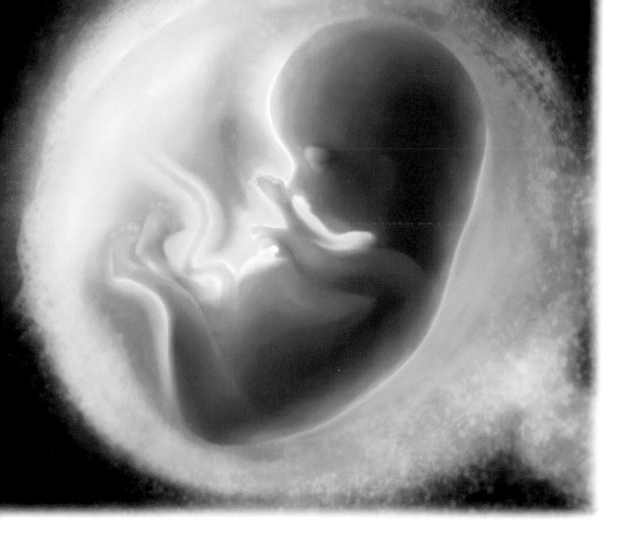

"One of the important subtle energies conveyed from the etheric is, of course, the life force. This influences the nucleus of every cell to carry out its specific activities."

subtle energies conveyed from the etheric is, of course, the life force. This influences the nucleus of every cell to carry out its specific activities. When the life force ceases to reach the nucleus, as at the time of death, the cell begins the process of breakdown into its chemical components.

Not surprisingly, blood is the symbol of life itself, and for many peoples its red color is considered to be sacred or highly auspicious.

The supply of blood from the mother provides the unborn child with life-sustaining substances for its vital organs.

The Respiratory System

The energy needed for the body's activities comes from burning food to release its energy. This requires oxygen, a gas that makes up about 20 percent of fresh air. Oxygen is drawn into the lungs when we inhale. The waste gas, carbon dioxide, which results from the burning process, is released when we exhale.

The lungs hang in the chest cavity, the walls of which are made up of the ribcage with the diaphragm forming the floor. The diaphragm is an upwardly arching sheet of muscle that flattens downward as we inhale. At the same time the muscles surrounding the ribs contract to lift them, widening and deepening the chest cavity. To exhale, the diaphragm muscle moves upward and the size of the chest cavity is decreased.

The rate of inhalation and exhalation depends on how quickly the body uses up the oxygen and how quickly it accumulates carbon dioxide. The respiratory center of the brain sends out the nervous impulse to the respiratory muscles. Other nerves monitor the levels of oxygen and carbon dioxide in the blood.

The transfer of oxygen and carbon dioxide into and from the blood is facilitated by the millions of tiny air sacs in the lungs, the alveoli, which are covered with a fine network of blood capillaries. The walls of the capillaries are so thin that gases can easily pass through them. Most of the oxygen we inhale combines chemically with the hemoglobin of the blood and is carried to the tissues. Here it is released again as oxygen. At the same time the blood picks

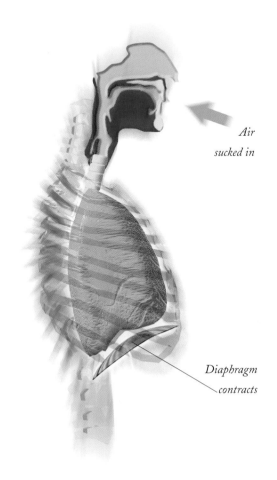

Air sucked in

Diaphragm contracts

up the carbon dioxide released by the tissue cells and returns it to the alveoli of the lungs to be exhaled.

The life force is present in air and, through respiration, is carried by the blood to the nucleus of every cell. This is the subtle role of respiration. The subtle function of the breath keeps us in touch with and reminds us of the Source.

Respiratory rate reveals our current state of being and is one of the first things the healer notices on meeting a client. Controlled breathing may be used to bring balance and harmony to the body, which in turn sets up an energetic impulse to bring the same

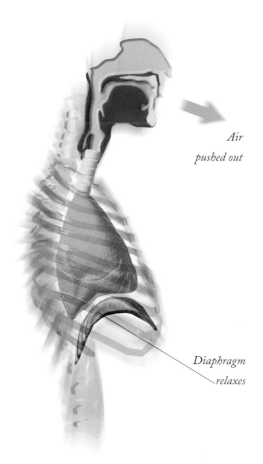

Air
pushed out

Inhalation and exhalation are
helped by the diaphragm; contracting
as we breathe in, and relaxing when
we breathe out.

Diaphragm
relaxes

harmony to the mind and emotions. Thus the breath and breathing are key therapeutic tools for the spiritual healer.

Most people's lifestyles do not encourage proper breathing. A sitting or slumped posture can lead to a habit of shallow breathing where half of the lungs' capacity is never used. Any form of exercise that speeds up the breathing rate for short periods will improve lung capacity and strengthen the heart.

A simple way to test whether you are breathing in the most efficient way is to sit or lie comfortably and relax. Now put one hand in the middle of your chest and the other in the middle of your belly. Breathe normally and notice which hand seems to move up and down the most. If it is the hand on your chest then your breathing is shallow. If it is the one on your belly, you are making the best use of the breath.

If you look at a baby as it lies on its back, notice the way that it breathes. The belly has the most movement, yet it is soft. This "soft belly" breathing, which we did during our early days on planet earth, is our most natural way of breathing and the one we need to get back to. The next exercise encourages you to experience a complete breath.

Exercise 8:
Full-Breath Breathing

1 Sit or lie in a comfortable position and relax. If sitting make sure that your feet are flat on the floor. Breathe normally. Put both hands on your belly and imagine that they are placed on a balloon. Now breathe in through the nose, slowly and deeply without straining, allowing the balloon to inflate, with the chest rising last of all.

2 Pause for a moment and then allow the balloon to deflate, slowly and gently without straining. The belly should be the last part of you to lower itself. Relax.

3 Now do the exercise six more times so that you become used to the sensation of breathing fully and deeply. If you are carrying out the exercise with a partner, discuss your experiences. The need to cough, for example, generally means that you are not used to breathing deeply. Are you in control of your breath? If so, how do you do this?

4 Another time, be conscious of the fact that you are breathing in the life force, the love of the Source. What happens when you take seven breaths in this way?

Now we will use the exercise to create a pattern of conscious breathing that increases lung capacity and gives a greater sense of control.

Exercise 9:
Rhythmic Breathing

1 Sit or lie comfortably as before. If sitting make sure that your feet are flat on the floor. Relax and breathe normally. You are going to take a full breath but this time to the count of four, slowly and deliberately. Hold your breath for the count of two, without straining.

2 Exhale to the count of four and count two again. This is one rhythmic cycle.

3 Repeat the cycle four more times, evenly and without straining.

4 When you feel you are quite comfortable with the four/two rhythm, inhale again, this time to the count of six. Hold your breath to the count of three. Exhale to the count of six. Count three before inhaling again.

5 Breathe rhythmically only within easily manageable limits. You should never strain. Clients can be taught to breathe more efficiently. Practice with a partner first before teaching someone else how to do a breathing exercise. Full-breath breathing aids digestion and sound sleep. It brings a sense of calm when you may be feeling stressed, depressed, or unhappy. It encourages a relaxed and stable center of gravity, which is below the navel.

The next exercise uses the human rainbow to bring balance to your energy field.

Exercise 10:
The Rainbow Breath

1 Stand with your feet about shoulder-width apart. Relax and breathe normally. Imagine that you are going to breathe seven spheres of colored light around you. Each sphere will balance that aspect of your aura.

2 See the color red in your mind's eye. As you inhale see a sphere of this light begin under your feet and extend up the front of your body to your head. As you exhale, the sphere continues to extend down the back of your body to complete the sphere of red light around you.

3 In your mind's eye see the color orange. Inhale, bringing up the sphere of orange light on the outside of the red sphere. Exhale to complete the orange sphere of light.

4 See the color golden yellow and create this color of light around the orange sphere in the same way as before.

5 Continue to breathe up green, blue, indigo, and violet light spheres around you. You have now cleared and balanced your aura. How does it feel? You can use this exercise any time that you need to balance the levels of energy in your energy field.

The Nervous System

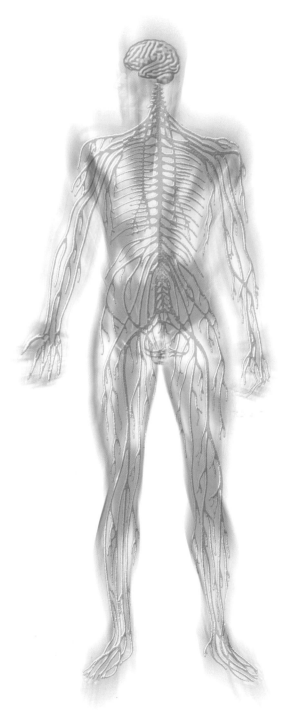

Even though breathing seems to be an automatic process, you were able to control it in the last three exercises. You sent a message to your brain that you would be in charge this time and that you wanted to modify the respiratory process for a period. All this was possible because of the body's nervous system, which can not only carry out operations without our having to ask but can also respond to our direct commands. This means that when you carry out conscious breathing you send a message to the mind that you are in charge.

The body's systems are controlled by the nervous system. Messages are transmitted by electrochemical impulses, with the brain acting as the command center. The network of nerves extending from the spinal cord to every organ and tissue enables the brain to monitor all the body's processes as well as monitor what is happening to us externally. The pattern of this network originates in the system of energy channels in the etheric body.

The autonomic part of the peripheral nervous system controls the internal environment of breathing, digestion, heart rate, and other physiological activities. It is as if these things happen automatically. At some level we are aware, but we do not need to have these functions at the front of our awareness.

The brain, housed in the bony skull, is the most important part of the body's nervous system and the center of our consciousness. As we explained earlier, even subtle events are processed in the brain so that our consciousness is not fragmented. The brain has three main sections—the cerebrum, the cerebellum, and the brain stem.

The largest part of the brain, the cerebrum, has two halves, or hemispheres, which reflect our dual nature. The left hemisphere tends to deal with logical thinking, analysis, linear, and linguistic/verbal issues. The right hemisphere tends to deal with creative thinking, artistic, esthetic, spatial, nonlinear, and intuitive events and issues. Some people are described as being more left- or right-brained, meaning that they have a tendency to favor one side over the other, which in turn influences the way they think and behave. To have a holistic view of ourselves, others, and the universe, we need to have a balanced development of both sides of our cerebrum.

The smaller cerebellum maintains the body's equilibrium and coordinates muscular activities. The brain stem links us with our relatives in the animal world. It includes the thalamus and hypothalamus, which regulate hunger, thirst, sleep, and sexual behavior; the midbrain, which transfers impulses from one part of the brain to another; and the medulla, which governs autonomic activities such as breathing, heart rate, and other vital functions.

There does not seem to be one particular center for learning in the brain, and memories are stored repeatedly in different parts. This has been shown when people who have lost brain tissue or the use of certain areas of the brain along with the memories that were stored there have later been able to relearn things and store the memories in other parts of the brain.

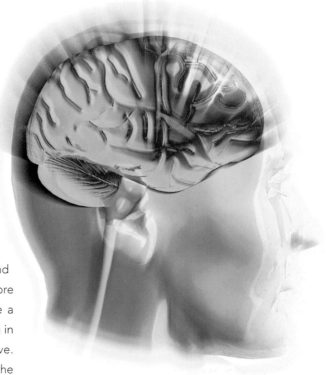

Your brain is an amazing instrument of great complexity, storing all your memories and thoughts.

How Nerves Send Messages

Every moment the brain receives information about what is going on internally and externally. But we pay little attention to these thousands of impulses unless they appear to be alarm signals. The brain receives and sends its messages using two kinds of energy—electrical and electrochemical. A message is moved along a nerve cell by electricity. But electricity cannot bridge the gap, or synapse, between one cell and another. This is done by a chemical neurotransmitter. Impulses being sent to the brain travel in exactly the same way.

The Endocrine System

The second of the body's major control systems is the series of endocrine glands that secrete chemical messages, in the form of hormones, directly into the bloodstream. Their messages can initiate, stop, slow down, or speed up a bodily process. All these reactions are triggered by the monitoring of the nervous system and of the brain.

The endocrine system, and the numerous functions of its glands, is of central importance to spiritual healers. It acts as the physical gateway for the energies of the etheric chakras, creating a special link between the body and all other levels of being. In this way, the endocrine glands not only perform a physical function but also receive and process a range of subtle energies that have a direct effect on these functions. This relationship is described on page 47. Bearing in mind these relationships, let us review the physical functions of the endocrine glands. Related chakras are shown in brackets.

In males, the testes (sacral) control sexual development and maturity, and the production of sperm. Sperm may carry an X or Y chromosome. If a Y chromosome fertilizes an egg the child will be male.

The ovaries (sacral) in females control sexual development and maturity, and the production of eggs. All eggs carry only the X chromosome.

The pancreas (solar plexus), and especially the groups of endocrine cells called the islets of Langerhans, control the level of sugar in the blood. This vital function even affects the brain, which needs the essential nutrient glucose.

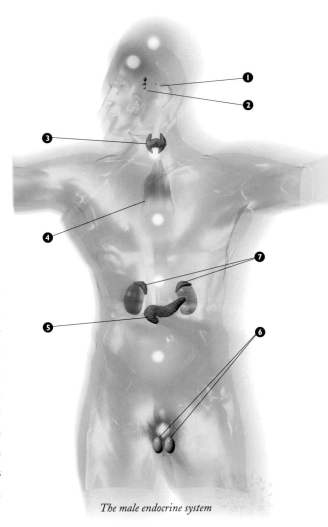

The male endocrine system

The adrenal glands (base) at the top of the kidneys control the salt and water balance in the body and help prepare it for emergencies. Important in personal survival, adrenaline speeds up heart and breathing rates and releases sugars in the muscles so that we can stand and fight or run away.

The thymus gland (heart) is responsible for the development of the immune system in infants, when it is relatively large. It produces cells called lymphocytes, which recognize the body's own tissues but will attack invading cells. Later, as the thymus

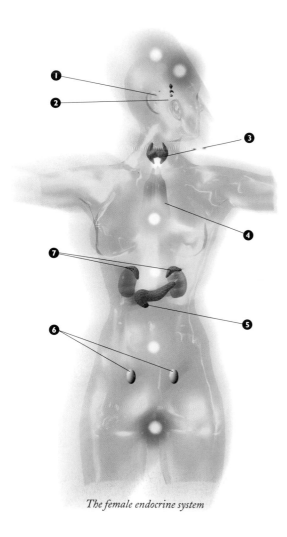

The female endocrine system

The endocrine glands and the chakras

	Gland	Related chakra
❶	pineal	crown
❷	pituitary/hypothalamus	brow
❸	thyroid	throat
❹	thymus	heart
❺	islets of Langerhans (pancreas)	solar plexus
❻	ovaries or testes	sacral
❼	adrenals	base

The brain stem organ, the hypothalamus, controls the secretions of the pituitary gland (brow), which in turn regulates the activity of the other endocrine glands. The hypothalamus communicates with the pituitary gland either by nerve impulses or by its own hormones. These stimulate the pituitary to secrete a range of hormones that have an effect on most of the body's functions, through the stimulation of other glands and organs.

The overseeing function of the pituitary in the physical body mimics the overseeing role of the brow chakra in the etheric body.

The pineal gland (crown) lies behind and above the hypothalamus. It is indirectly sensitive to light and secretes melatonin when light begins to fade and during the darker part of the year. In this way the pineal gland enables us to appreciate the rhythm of day and night and the passing of the seasons. However, we may become depressed by too many gray days and develop seasonal affective disorder (SAD). Spiritual healers have also noticed a similar syndrome induced in clients by too many gray or negative patterns of thinking.

It is perhaps no coincidence that the topmost gland of the system is affected by light and informs the body about light, for this is where the spiritual light of the crown center enters the body at a subtle level.

reduces in size, the lymph nodes, bone marrow, and spleen take over this role. In adulthood the thymus continues to play its subtle role of conducting heart chakra energies, effectively providing a link between our immune system and its capabilities and our response to love issues.

The thyroid gland (throat) controls the body's metabolism and rate of growth. The parathyroids, embedded in the thyroid gland, control the level of calcium in the blood. The skeleton has a subtle link with the throat chakra through these glands.

What the Chakra Colors May Reveal

From our study of the chakras and the endocrine glands you will appreciate that both short- and long-term conditions have an energetic effect. This is detected in the chakras when they are scanned by the healer. Energetic effects are revealed to sensitive awareness, especially to inner vision.

You will recall that in Exercise 6, "Sensing Color in the Major Chakras" (see page 31), you attempted to detect colors in each chakra and that they very often varied from the balancing color. This discrepancy is highlighted in the case of a specific condition. For example, a healer may not be able to sense the color sky blue in a person with a sore throat.

When the subtle links to a condition are obvious or understood, the situation may be greatly improved by directing the appropriate color of light to the chakra concerned. In the case of the sore throat, the main color needed would be blue. If the throat condition was compounded by congested lungs, it would also be appropriate to direct the color green to the heart chakra.

The healer needs to be alert to the whole person and what is going on in his or her life. Assumptions should never be made about what needs to be done for a person, but in the energetic diagnosis stage of the work, the healer should be aware of the signals given off by the physical and etheric bodies. This may well inform how the healing routine is to be conducted. Because a healer's perceptions are subjective, they should not be conveyed to the client.

A case of eczema on the hands will illustrate the point. The arms are related to the heart chakra and so are the hands. But when something happens to the hands such as eczema, another chakra may be at work. As you look at a standing person you will see that the hands are opposite the base chakra. In many cases of eczema, especially in children, their feelings of safety, security, or their very survival, may for some reason be undermined. The healing scan would confirm that healing energy was needed in the base center as well as the heart. Here, the color red is needed as well as green.

Remember that spiritual healing is a complementary therapy and should not take the place of medical help or attention. However, the client may direct color to a chakra as a self-healing strategy through a simple breathing exercise.

Exercise 11:
Breathing Color to Balance
the Chakras

1 Sit or lie comfortably, relax, and breathe normally. If sitting make sure your feet are flat on the floor. Neither your arms nor your legs should be crossed. Your intention is to breathe a color into the chakras.

2 Put your mind in the crown chakra. In your mind's eye see the color violet as a light. Do not worry if you are unsuccessful in "seeing" since your mental intention will make sure that the work is done. Now imagine that you can breathe a violet light into the crown chakra. Slowly and gently breathe this light into the crown chakra, without straining. You may feel the chakra needs a second breath of color in order to be sufficiently filled.

3 Let your mind slip down to the brow chakra. See the color indigo or royal blue. It should be without traces of darkness. If it is, lighten it. Breathe the color into the chakra, slowly and gently.

4 Put your mind in the throat, heart, solar plexus, sacral, and base chakras, breathing in the balancing lights of blue, green, golden yellow, orange, and red respectively.

5 Note any sensations and/or changes you experience. The exercise concludes at the base chakra in order to leave you fully grounded.

With a partner, this exercise could be combined with Exercise 6, "Sensing Color in the Major Chakras" (see page 31). Make sure that you keep a note of your experiences and discuss them together.

> Make sure that you can accurately recall the balanced colors of the chakras. You may find it helpful to record this exercise and play it back for your use or to get a partner to read it to you.

Using the Breath to Improve Vitality and Maintain Harmony

We have explored how the chakras reveal the state of our energy field through their color vibrations. These states are generally created by our own activities and thoughts, and they are areas of being for which we can start to take responsibility. Part of our responsibility to ourselves is to monitor our energy levels. Are they being depleted and if so how? Human company involves mixing with other people's auras. A law of energy balance is that anyone who is low in energy will tend to absorb energy from others. This becomes especially evident when we are in crowded places such as supermarkets or shopping malls.

"A law of energy balance is that anyone who is low in energy will tend to absorb energy from others."

Spiritual healers need to be conscious of energy transactions so that they can give energy to another when they want to but not have it taken from them. In the meantime their energy levels need to be maintained at a high level and in a harmonious state. Many of the self-healing exercises, such as Exercises 10 and 11 (pages 43 and 49), will help you to do this. Emergency maintenance can be carried out with the next two exercises.

Exercise 12: Breathing in Vitality Energy

As well as the life force, we all need vitality energy, especially if we lead demanding lives and have jobs that require high energy levels. There are two types of vitality that originate from the cosmos and are beamed to us via the sun. These have the general colors of orange and yellow. They may be breathed into the appropriate chakra to increase vitality levels and energize the body and its systems.

Orange Vitality Energy

It is good to face the sun, or the direction of the sun, but not essential.

1 Stand with your legs shoulder-width apart and the arms relaxed. Or sit comfortably with the feet flat on the floor. Breathe normally and focus on your feet, realizing that they are your connection to the planet.

2 Now slowly bring your focus to the sacral chakra. Imagine that you can breathe a special vitality energy from the sun into this chakra. It has the color orange. It does not matter if you cannot see this color; simply affirm your mental intention.

Yellow Vitality Energy

3 Inhale through the nose, drawing the orange vitality energy into your sacral chakra. It floods in and illuminates the sacral chakra, moving out into your whole body to vitalize it. It also energizes and balances all the organs that make up the the sacral region. This energy is particularly important for women since the feminine power center is in the sacral chakra.

4 Where there may have been problems in this area of the body, or emotional upsets, use the out-breath to let go of these energies that no longer serve you. You may need to take a number of breaths in order to vitalize the whole body, but the number of breaths that you take should not exceed seven.

1 The second level of vitality has the color golden yellow. Prepare yourself in the same way as before. This time bring your focus to the solar plexus chakra. Imagine that you can breathe the special golden yellow vitality energy from the sun into this chakra.

2 Allow the yellow energy to vitalize all the organs around the solar plexus and then to move out into the whole body.

3 Where there may have been problems in this area of the body or reactions of fear, anxiety, dislike, poor self-image, or lack of confidence, let go of these energies now as you exhale. Breathe out slowly and gently, positively letting go and allowing renewal.

Preparing for Healing

You have studied the etheric and physical body from the point of view of spiritual healing and practiced a number of exercises that have helped you to access the subtle levels of your being through working with the body. You are becoming familiar with the way that you sense subtle energies and with the levels of your awareness. By keeping a record of your sensations and experiences, and by comparing notes with a partner, you are creating your own database so that you can monitor your progress and developing awareness.

This early work of learning and experience helps build confidence in the reality and effects of healing energies, the confidence you will need to work with another person, knowing that you are working from the heart.

Part of your confidence will come from having thoroughly prepared yourself and the healing space for the work at hand. The healer's preparation is a form of attunement or opening to the energies of healing, the energies of the Source. These are available at all times, but we are rarely in a state of mind that is open to them. There is a number of ways to create your own healing channel and the healing state of mind. Since these methods effectively help you to create a healing lifestyle, we describe them in detail in Chapter 6: Creating the Channel.

The second area of preparation is the healing space itself which, by attunement to the work, becomes sacred space.

All our preparations will be to no avail, however, if we are unable to relax or if we worry about outcomes. This conveys a message to the client that we do not trust ourselves and we do not trust the healing. The relaxed healer creates a healing atmosphere. The relaxed client is in the best possible state to absorb and work with the energies.

So we begin the process of preparation by looking at the relaxation of body and mind.

Relaxation and Stress: Stress Effects

Anxiety generally heightens our response to a crisis, giving us the strength and focus to cope with situations such as an illness, a lost job, accident, or disaster. One of our responses to stressful situations of any kind is the stimulation of the adrenals. This helps the body to galvanize us into activity. Problems come when a person undergoes prolonged stress and the body has to deal with greater and greater amounts of stress-produced chemicals in the blood. If you have to drive to work every day, the chances are that you experience stress in the form of anxiety, fear, anger, and impatience. When regular stress cannot be adequately dealt with, as in the situation caused by driving in heavy traffic, the body will begin to signal that this is not a good way to live.

"But as soon as we can relieve the early symptoms through activities such as dedicated exercise, gardening, a pastime, or leisure pursuit, we move into a more relaxed mode of being and the body is able to regain its balance."

Stress response speeds up our breathing and heart rate, slows down digestion and excretion, and releases sugars in the muscles. Stress may also encourage us to seek solace in eating more than the body needs, to smoke, drink alcohol, or take drugs. It is easy to see how the person who is unable to regain harmony within the body may develop a condition linked to these stress responses such as heart disease or a dependence on harmful drugs.

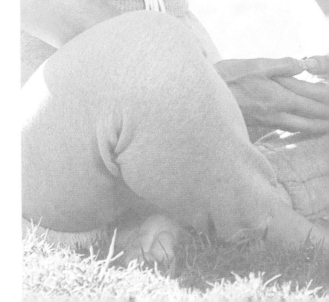

Controlling your breathing will help to control stress. Full-breath breathing will make you feel centered and control your focus.

Relaxation Effects

One of the simplest ways of combating stress is to relax the body and control the breath. Both these forms of control send a message to the mind that you are taking charge of certain automatic activities such as breathing, heart rate, and muscle tension. The feeling of taking charge brings in turn a sense of calmness and centeredness. When someone is urged to calm down, it would help if she was also encouraged to breathe slowly and deeply. This simple act immediately slows down mental activity so that the person is able to feel that she has control of herself once more.

When under stress, practice full-breath breathing until you feel centered. Then put your focus either in your center of gravity, the sacral center, or in the heart center. When a sense of grounding and solidity is needed, focus on your center of gravity in the sacral: to take yourself out of the fear place of the solar plexus, focus on the heart center. To aid your focus begin to breathe into either of these chakras.

Relaxation of the body begins with the breath but has to take place also in the muscles, skeleton, and nerves—in effect, the whole of the body. Here, every muscle is systematically put into a state of relaxation. Gradually tension begins to leave the various systems and the skeleton itself is allowed to regain its true form. In time, you will find that improved digestion and sounder sleep return to the body.

When confronted by any kind of stress we tend to tense up. This may range from simply screwing up our eyes, a nervous twitch or gesture to a collapse or doubling over of the body. Similarly, if we are feeling, or about to feel, pain, the body goes into a state of tension. This may trigger further pain. These are all problems that can be resolved by practicing relaxation, either in a localized area or throughout the whole body.

Relaxation then is a healing tool we need as practitioners and can teach to our clients. It can become part of our lifestyle just as it is part of the preparation for every healing session.

Exercise 13:
Full Body Relaxation

You will find it helpful to tape this exercise or to have a partner read it to you. Proceed at a gentle pace, allowing plenty of time for the activity.

1 Practice this exercise for the first time with your shoes off and lie on your back on the floor. If this is not possible find the most comfortable position that you can. Breathe normally.

2 This exercise is about feeling the tension within your body and getting to know the feeling of its leaving and allowing your body to resume its natural form. This process is called relaxation. Close your eyes so that you can focus on your sensations and experiences.

3 Clench your fists as tightly as you can. Unclench them slowly, noticing the feeling of relaxing and letting go. Now coordinate this action with the breath. As you inhale slowly and gently, clench your fists and hold that tension for a moment. As you exhale, unclench, relax, and let go, allowing the tension to leak away.

4 Practice this one more time. Breathe in, clenching the fists and holding the tension for a moment. Breathe out, unclenching, relaxing, and letting go with the out-breath. Remember the feeling of unclenching and relaxing. Do not tense any muscle or part of your body from now on. Breathe normally. Know in your mind that you are breathing in peace and breathing out any stress, anxieties, or problems.

5 Put your mind in your left foot. Allow each toe to unclench, one by one. Move slowly over the arch of your foot, relaxing the muscles. Combine your relaxation with your out-breath. Let go as you breathe out. Let the ankle joint relax. Move up your left leg, relaxing the muscles, letting go as you breathe out. Relax the knee joint. Unclench the thigh muscles and the muscles of the buttocks. Let them relax.

6 Move across the pelvis, allowing it to relax as you breathe out.

7 Focus on your right foot. Allow each toe to unclench, one by one. Move slowly over the arch of your foot, relaxing the muscles. Let the ankle joint relax as you breathe out.

8 Move up your right leg, relaxing the muscles. Relax the knee joint as you breathe out. Unclench the thigh muscles and the muscles of the buttocks. Relax the pelvis again.

9 Now move up the front of the body, relaxing the belly and stomach as you breathe out. Relax the chest muscles. Let go of the shoulders as you breathe out.

10 Allow yourself to return to the pelvis and slowly relax the muscles of the back on both sides of the spine. Let go of the muscles at the back of the shoulders as you breathe out.

11 Relax the left shoulder and move down the left arm. Relax the elbow joint. Move down the forearm and relax the wrist. Relax the palm and the fingers and thumb, one by one.

12 Return to the right shoulder. Relax it and move down the right arm. Relax the elbow. Move down the forearm and relax the wrist. Relax the palm, the fingers, and thumb.

13 As you relax the whole shoulder girdle, focus on the back of your neck. Move up your neck, slowly, allowing the neck to relax totally as you breathe out. Move up the back of the head and over the top of the scalp, relaxing and letting go of the tiny muscles.

14 Now imagine that a caring hand gently smooths your forehead. Your eyes relax, also the cheeks and mouth. Your jaw unclenches. You smile a slow, relaxed smile and you feel generally relaxed .

15 Stay in this relaxed state, breathing normally. Scan your body all over to see if any part has tensed up again. If it has, unclench it once more. Enjoy the feeling of total relaxation. You can remain mentally alert or drift off to sleep.

16 When you are ready to resume other activities, become aware of your body. Wiggle your hands and toes. Smooth yourself with your hands. This makes sure that you have returned to your body. Sit up slowly. Make sure that your eyes are focused before getting up. If you are with a partner, discuss your experiences.

Do not worry if you drift off to sleep during this exercise. Use it to induce sound sleep.
Some people like to do this exercise to the accompaniment of soothing music. Make sure that there are no disturbing gaps or loud noises to interrupt the flow. With practice you will be able to relax your body in any situation. Your energies will flow to a new, calmer rhythm as they move into a state of balance. This is why relaxation is the essence of healing.

Mental Relaxation

Our mental perception of events and situations triggers the stress response in the body, so we also need to be able to relax the mind. Finding ways to understand and modify our own mental conditioning will become part of our personal development program, but in the meantime we can use emergency relaxation methods such as the following exercise.

Exercise 14:
A Walk to Relax the Mind

You will find it helpful to tape this exercise or to have a partner read it to you. Again, proceed at a gentle pace, allowing time for the mental activities. The physical setting of the walk should be modified to suit the person, the environment, and culture. Here, we describe a journey that has a setting adapted for Western cultures.

1 Sit comfortably with your feet flat on the floor and the hands resting on the thighs, palms-up. You could also lie down. Relax your body and breathe normally. In your imagination you are going to take a short walk that will soothe and balance your mind.

2 Become aware of your breath and focus on the sound of your breathing for a few breaths. Now let your mind rest. You are out in the country, walking easily along a lane. The sun is shining and you feel at ease and happy within yourself.

3 As the lane gently rises you feel a slight breeze on your cheeks from time to time. Trees move gently in this breeze. As you glance to either side of the lane you see animals in the fields. The sight of them seems to increase your feeling of peace and contentment.

4 Ahead you see an opening with a gate. It is the gate to a beautiful garden. You know you are invited in, so you quietly open the gate and enter the garden. For a moment you stop to look at the shrubs and flowers, noticing their shapes and colors. Then you see a bench and make your way to it.

5 Sitting on the bench, time seems to stand still. You have no cares or worries. It is as if being here in the garden has put all the facets of your life into perspective. What matters is the beauty of your surroundings and the beauty you sense inside yourself. Birds sing. Insects buzz. You hear the distant sound of someone working patiently on the land. You decide to stay a while on this bench, simply relaxed and enjoying the moment.

6 Now you realize it is time to go and make your way back to the gate, taking a last look at the garden as you pass. You open and close the gate and find yourself in the tree-lined lane once more.

7 You set off back down the lane, remembering the same trees as you pass them, remembering the same animals in the fields. Your step is jaunty. This walk and the time in the garden have refreshed you at a very deep level. You feel ready to tackle anything now.

8 The lane has brought you back to where you are sitting. Spend a few moments with your feelings.

9 Get in touch with your body and rub your hands together before you stand up.

We recommend that you carry out the relaxation exercises with a partner so that you get practice in teaching another person how to relax both physically and mentally. With this aim in mind perhaps you can devise your own methods. When the client comes for healing, after checking the breathing, the healer checks the person's state of relaxation. If necessary, you may need to teach the client how to relax before you attempt to give healing. This should be seen as part of the client's attunement.

Personal Attunement

Having experienced the role of the breath and relaxation in bringing about balance, you are ready to bring that state of balance to the practice of spiritual healing. This is done through personal attunement.

Attunement, in the sense used in spiritual healing, means tuning ourselves into, or making ourselves open to, the energies of healing at every level of our being. This means remembering that all energy emanates from the Source and is the Source.

First find out what helps you to focus the mind and body in preparation for work as a healer. It could be lighting a candle, which is a simple and beautiful symbol of the Light. It could be listening to certain music, burning incense, saying a prayer, beating a drum. Whatever helps you is a sure aid in beginning your process of attunement.

As we discovered in Chapter 1, all living things radiate a constantly changing field of energy. Energies have been absorbed by buildings and the furniture within them. They are present in the environment we inhabit, whether this is a busy city or remote countryside. From their initial presence in our aura, our thoughts and emotions move out into the universal field wherever we go.

"In our everyday life it is natural for us to absorb various energies, some of which are beneficial while others are not. The first step in attunement is to clear the personal energy field of all energies that have accumulated in it."

Exercise 15:
Clearing the Energy Field

1 Stand with the feet shoulder-width apart, or sit with your feet flat on the floor. Relax your body, with the hands unjoined. Breathe normally through the nose.

2 The light that clears is silver. Imagine that you can breathe this light into your energy field and into your body as you stand under a cascade of silver light. Allow the light to flow out of every orifice and out of every finger and toe.

3 Gradually, the energies within your body begin to clear. See if you can detect a fresh new color of light that enters.

4 The silver light is flowing through your energy field, clearing it and allowing a new light to fill it. Allow the clearing to continue until you feel cleansed inside and out. You are breathing quite normally all this time, but do not forget that during the out-breath you can let go of any energies, thoughts, or memories that no longer serve you.

If you intuitively feel the need for further harmonization of your energies, carry out Exercise 10, "The Rainbow Breath" (see page 43).

Remember, silver is the light of cleansing and clearing. You can use this color with mental intention to clear objects and places of old energies. Just acknowledge your personal responsibility for your own actions, including your mental actions.

You have now reached a point of energetic balance where you are ready to consider your relationship with the Source. This is the same relationship as that with your soul. Once more you recall that you are a soul with a body, and the body is about to work on behalf of the soul. Entering into the silence of this presence, or meditation, is the most effective state of communion. You may also want to reinforce your connection through prayer—to give thanks for the opportunity to be of service, to ask that soul should guide the work, to ask for protection for yourself and the client, to dedicate the work to all beings, and so on. Whatever you need to do to be at one with the soul is your preparation.

Attuning the Healing Space

Having brought yourself into a state of connection with the sacred, you are ready to prepare the room so that its atmosphere is conducive to healing, safe and welcoming to the client, and a pleasure for you to work in.

First assess the general feel of the room. It needs to be bright and airy, warm, clean, uncluttered, comfortable but businesslike. Flowers always add a special welcoming energy to a room; in fact, they may be treated as sacred offerings. There should be water and tissues within easy reach. A healing couch and a chair for the healing sessions, as well as two chairs positioned so that you and the client can talk with each other, are essential furniture.

You are now ready to attune the room. First, if you have not already done so, it should be cleared of any previous energies so that you and your client are starting with a clear energetic environment. Next, this environment should be balanced. The intention is to create a sacred space and, according to a law of energy, energy follows thought.

Of course, you can clear and balance a room in the same way that you cleared and balanced your own self. You could visualize silver light flooding the room, moving into every corner, and then carrying the old energies outside where the planet and the sun will help these energies to disperse and become neutral in force once more. You will then have to check with your awareness that fresh new energies arrive to fill the space. This you can achieve with practice.

There are many other ways to attune the healing space, which may remind you of what goes on in a

"We do not want riches. We want peace and love."
Native American leader, Red Cloud, 1870

temple or church where traditions of clearing and balancing date back to ancient times. These include taking the light of the candle into all parts of the room, a method common among the Native Americans of the Canadian west coast. Or you could use the sound of clapping hands, a bell, rattle, drum, or the voice; or use smoke from a dedicated source such as incense or herbs to clear and balance the area. The important thing is the mental intention and the dedication of the method before starting. Perhaps you can realize that the power of our very thoughts may bring the sacred into any space just as they can create an atmosphere of negativity.

The things we can do, the rituals and ceremonies, are physical ways to reconnect with the sacred and powerful reminders of what we are trying to achieve. They can make our preparations fun, colorful, prayerful, and a pleasure to carry out. Finally, the next exercise unites us with the space.

Exercise 16: Breathing Love and Peace

1 Sit in a chair in the healing room with your feet flat on the floor. Relax the body with your hands resting palms-up on the thighs (the palms-up position allows you to be aware of energies outside yourself). Take three slow full breaths.

2 Love is harmony on all levels. It is not something we have to do but a way of being. Imagine you can breathe in the energy of love. You may see this as the color pink. Using the full breath, breathe in love, allowing

it to fill every part of your body. Let go of any unloving thoughts or feelings of fear or anxiety on the out-breath.

3 Continue to breathe love gently in, letting it fill your aura and then move out into the healing room.

4 Peace is wholeness on all levels of our being. It is not merely the absence of strife. Just like love, peace is a creative energy that is the manifestation of wholeness. Imagine that you can breathe in the energy of peace. This may appear to you as a color such as white, pink, or blue. Breathe in peace, filling the body. On the out-breath, let go of any disturbing or hostile feelings or any desperate need for peace to prevail (this is a fear-based feeling).

5 Allow the energy of peace to fill the aura and then to move out into the room.

6 Sense the atmosphere of love and peace that you have created within you and that fills the room. Spend some moments realizing that this is the atmosphere you have created for your clients. This is where they will have their healing experience.

Are You a Healer?

Before reading this book you may have had feelings that urged you to reach out to help another. Sometimes you may have sensed that someone needed your help and you knew where to put your hands. Or you may be working as a healer already and just need some confirmation that you are on the right track. Get used to trusting your inner feelings. Find ways of confirming them before you seek the opinion of others. Your reliance on your intuition and your common sense is essential if you are to develop as a healer.

Here is a way to find out if your inner promptings have any foundation. The following exercises should be tried before learning a healing method. They may follow your process of personal attunement.

Exercise 17: Attunement to Another Person

You will need a partner, or ideally, a group of friends who are happy to let you experiment. None of you should have exchanged any information about how you are feeling at the time or about any condition that any of you might be experiencing. Divide into pairs.

1 Sit opposite each other and relax. Breathe normally. Close your eyes and focus on your heart center. Imagine that as you breathe your heart center begins to open. Feel its energy flowing into your body and then flowing out toward your partner.

2 With your focus gently in your own heart center, allow yourself to absorb any impressions about your partner. These may be feelings, pictures, colors, etc. Do not seize on them to try to understand them and do not pass any judgment on them. Simply absorb them into yourself.

3 Sit together in this way for two to four minutes. Then open your eyes and make a note of your impressions about your partner. Do not exchange information; you will need it later. Proceed to the next exercise.

Exercise 18:
Attunement to Healing

Stay with the same partner. Take the role of healer while your partner becomes the client. The client can choose to stand, sit, or lie on a healing couch if there is one available. For the purpose of the exercise, your partner should keep her eyes open.

1 Take a few full breaths to center yourself. Relax and breathe normally. Focus on your hands. Where do they want to go to help your client? Let them go there, holding them a few inches away from the client's body. Keep them at this place until you feel the need to withdraw them or to move them to another place.

2 Bearing in mind what you sensed during the earlier attunement exercise, do you need to work anywhere else?

3 Finally signal to your client that you have completed your work and step back. If your client has changed consciousness, help her back into her body by asking her to wiggle her toes and shake her hands. Check her eyes to see that they focus properly.

Well, do you feel you may be a healer now? Your innate abilities, your link with other people and with the sacred will always be the foundation of your work, so you will need to find a place for them in any healing method you may learn.

Now sit together. Compare experiences from both attunement exercises. What confirmation did you receive from your partner that your attunement and intuition were working?

The Healing Experience

It is possible to learn how to carry out a healing session, but the urge of the soul to give service to others (whether they be human, animal, plant, the environment, or a situation) is a function of the heart rather than the mind. So you need to listen to your inner voice and consciously develop a relationship with the Source and the spiritual realms, to open the heart and free your innate talent for caring and healing. (See also Chapter 6: Creating the Channel).

Once you are satisfied that spiritual healing is a way in which you can offer your light to the world it may be time to train, to work with others, or to join an organization dedicated to healing. Take your time, have a good look around, and choose carefully. Listen to the comments and recommendations of others, but listen most of all to your own inner voice. Only you know what resonates and what feels really right for you. A professional body will make sure that you are properly insured, that you have a safe method of working, and that you will adhere to a professional code of conduct—safeguards for the public as much as for yourself. See pages 142–143 for some useful addresses.

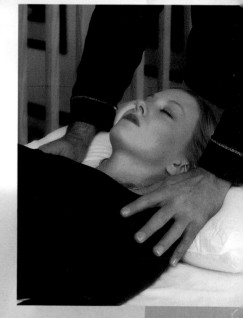

In this chapter I set out a proven method of working that is safe, effective, and thorough. It can serve as a framework for your own intuitive way. Make sure that, as well as working with as many other people as possible, you undergo the personal experience of healing so that you understand what a client can expect.

This book will will be even more effective in conjunction with a loving mentor. Choose your mentor carefully. Notice whether your mentor's teaching or comments empower you or leave you with a feeling of inferiority.

You have chosen to read this book because you know you have something to offer others. Perhaps it will be the healing experience.

"Helping hands are holier than lips that pray." *Sathya Sai Baba, Indian avatar.*

Meeting the Client

Source

universal
energy field

oneness

patient — healer

—— permanent link
------ temporary link
⟩ attunement
⟩⟩ flow of healing energy

The Healing Triangle comes into effect through your personal
attunement and attunement to your client.

Having prepared yourself and the healing space, you are now ready to meet your client. This person may never have met you before and yet is expected to put himself entirely in your hands. This trust needs to be respected and your respect for the client must be demonstrated. He needs to be assured that everything that takes place in the healing session is confidential and that he can be himself without being judged. "How can I help?" is a better question than "What's the problem?"

Ask if the client has ever had spiritual healing before. You must be able to explain what you do in simple language and answer any questions without feeling defensive or threatened. As he sits opposite you, remember that the process of attunement with the client has begun. Your relaxed but attentive listening will enable you to gain many intuitive and psychic impressions that you may use to enhance your work later on in the session.

Being a good listener is a way of healing in itself—we all need someone to talk to and especially someone who will listen to us. To be able to listen with empathy to your client as part of the healing session is a skill you may want to develop. This can be done by training in person-centered counseling (see Useful Addresses on pages 142–43). Counseling skills will enhance your work, giving both you and your client more confidence. They also help to open up the client's energy field to healing.

During this first stage of the session you should be observing your client carefully and asking yourself questions. Most of what we communicate to each other is presented via the body and not through what we say, so what is the body saying to you? Is it distressed, defensive, rigid, out of shape, twitching, etc.? In fact, is the body saying one thing while the

"Being a good listener is a way of healing in itself—we all need someone to talk to and especially someone who will listen to us."

client's words say something else? How is the client breathing and is he relaxed enough? Someone who is in distress should be helped to carry out a simple breathing exercise to help him gain control. He may need to relax the body fully before he is in a fit state to receive healing. This will all be a natural part of the healing session, but your impressions of the client should be kept to yourself. They are your perceptions of the client and may not be how the client sees himself.

You should check whether a doctor has been consulted about the condition. Remind the client that spiritual healing is a complementary therapy and not an alternative. If the client is suffering from a reportable or infectious disease, he must be advised to see a doctor immediately and not permitted to come into contact with other clients. A list of these diseases can be obtained from your doctor or health center.

Your personal attunement and your attunement to the client have set up two sides of the Healing Triangle. This activates the third side, which is the client's own link with the Source. By activating this third side the client's own ability to heal himself is accessed.

Through practice you will sense when the Healing Triangle is in position. From this moment your job will be to maintain your link with the soul so that the work is directed from this level. You do not have to worry about what to do or what the outcome will be and, at some level, your client is aware of this.

Eye glasses should be removed, but only an overcoat or footwear needs to be taken off when the client is on the healing couch. Some people like to remove jewelry.

The presented condition should be borne in mind when offering either a chair or the couch.

Ask if your client objects to being touched and explain that it is not necessary, but that you do use touch to signal the beginning and end of the healing procedure. Sometimes you may feel intuitively that your client needs the reassurance of touch, but this should only occur with the client's consent.

The Healing Procedure

Healing on a Couch

This is the most comfortable way to work and the most comfortable position for most clients and for most conditions. Make sure that you have access to as many sides of the couch as possible. Check that the couch is stable and that all fittings are secured.

Before working with a client you should be thoroughly conversant with the following exercise. When it is used as a healing procedure it should always be preceded by your full attunement. To familiarize you with the healing procedure, we will call your partner the "client."

The first part of the procedure is the chakra scan. This sensing of each chakra allows you to assess its energetic state while it also absorbs or releases energy, according to the needs of the person at the time. The scan is followed by the balancing of the polarity channels.

The second part of the procedure is the skeletal scan. This sensing of the skeleton and its energy circuits allows you to assess its energetic state while it also absorbs or releases energy, according to its needs. The skeletal scan is followed by the balancing of the energy circuits.

The third part of the procedure relates to the reason why the client has come for healing. You may now need to return to a particular chakra or part of the body that may still be calling for healing. Your action will also reassure the client that you have heard what she has said. Begin with the highest vibration (a chakra) and work to the lowest (the body). This helps the client return to the body and prepares her for leaving the couch. Before learning the two healing scans, refresh your memory about the position of the chakras and the structure of the skeleton; for the scans follow the etheric and physical body plans.

"The sensing of each chakra allows you to assess its energetic state while it also absorbs or releases energy, according to the needs of the person at the time."

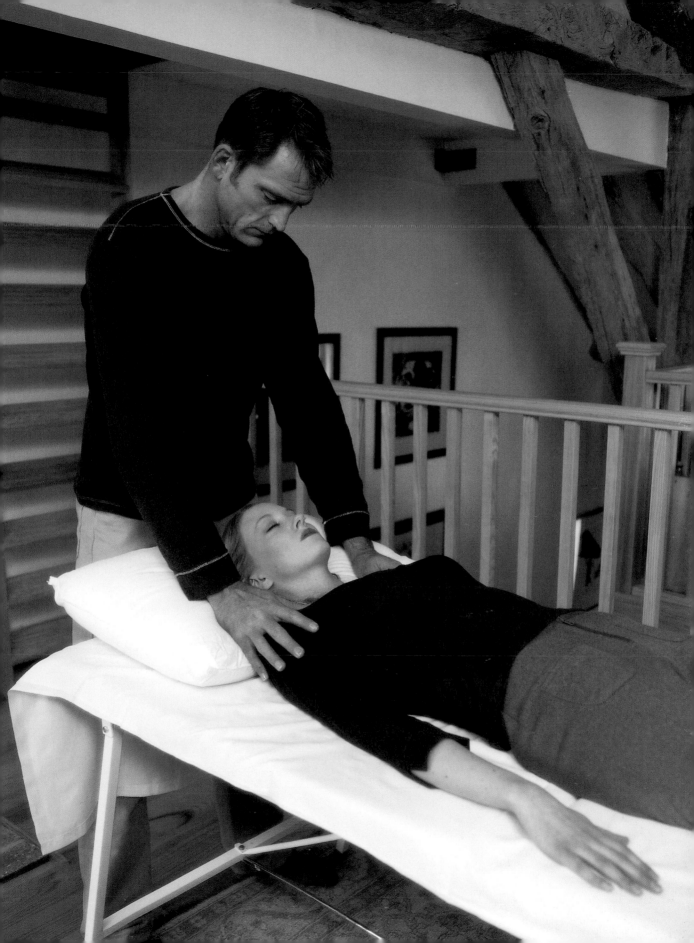

Exercise 19:
Healing with the Client
on a Couch

You will find it helpful to tape the exercise or to have it read aloud to you.

The Chakra Scan

1 Help the client to get onto the couch by supporting the back. Make sure that she is comfortable with a pillow under the head. For some back conditions, you may need to place another pillow under the raised knees. Make sure that there are no crossed limbs. Ask the client if she needs a blanket to cover her. Some people find this cover reassuring and comforting. Tell her that your signal for beginning the healing procedure will be a light touch on the shoulders. You will also use this same touch to signal that the procedure is over.

2 Stand a step away from the client's head, relax, and center yourself. Recall the link between your hands and your heart chakra. Mentally thank the client for this opportunity to work with her and ask that your two souls direct the healing. This continues your attunement with the client.

3 Step up to the client and gently place your hands on her shoulders. You may feel the movement of energy in your hands at this point.

Raise your hands up about 2–3 feet (60–90 cm) opposite the client's crown chakra, about head-width apart, with the palms sloping slightly inward. Gently move your hands toward the crown chakra until you feel a resistance from it. Stop and allow an interchange of energy. Note in what part of the aura your hands need to be. This is the level (mental or emotional) at which energy is needed. Note also whether energy is leaving your hands or vibrating against them. Move them toward the crown a little more if the feeling of resistance allows, but do not touch the crown of the head.

4 Step to one side of the client; and for this exercise, assume that you are standing at the client's right side. Keep your left hand at the crown chakra while you move your right hand to hold it above the brow chakra. Sense that you are gently moving energy toward the brow with your right palm. Lower your right hand until you feel the energetic resistance from the brow chakra. Stop and allow an interchange of energy. Again, note where you are in the client's aura and the sensations in your hands. Lower your right hand a little farther if possible. Keep an eye on the state of the client and her breathing. You now have your left hand at the crown while your right is at the brow chakra.

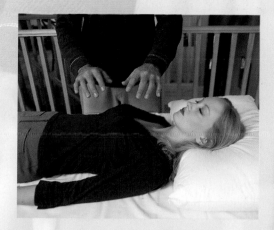

plexus chakra. Bring your left hand to the solar plexus chakra and move your right until it is over the sacral chakra. Bring your left hand to the sacral chakra and move your right until it is over the base chakra. Bring your left hand to the base chakra.

5 When you feel ready, bring your left hand to the brow so that it is at the same level as your right hand. Move your right hand until it is above the throat chakra and proceed in the same way. You now have data about the relationship between the three chakras. The leading hand is clearing and sensing while the other hand is making available the energies that are needed. The movements of the scan as described ensure that each chakra comes into balance and that they are in a state of mutual harmony.

6 Bring your left hand to the throat chakra. Move the right hand again until it is over the heart chakra. Proceed in the same way, being aware and sensitive with each slow and gentle movement. Take time to assess what you are experiencing.

7 Bring your left hand to the heart chakra and move the right hand until it is over the solar

8 Now move around to the client's feet to assess the balance of the two complementary subtle-energy streams. Recall Exercise 5, "Checking Polarity Balance" (page 30). Stand opposite the feet and hold your palms out toward the soles about 6–12 inches (15–30 cm) away from them. Sense the flow of energies between your hands and the client's soles. Hold your hands in this position until you sense that the energy flow is in balance.

This completes the chakra healing scan. You now have a diagnostic picture of the client at a subtle-energetic level. How does it relate to the client's story and to any impressions that you may have received? This is your perception and should not be conveyed to the client.

Recall that the chakras impact on the physical body through the endocrine glands and from there to the various organs and tissues. In this way, the chakra scan also works with the organs and tissues of the body.

The Skeletal Scan

1 For the skeletal healing scan return to your position at the client's head. Recall the illustration of the skeleton and its energy circuits on page 37. Your intention is to work with these circuits and with the skeletal system. Check that your client is still relaxed and breathing normally. If she has gone to sleep this is fine, do not wake her. Check your own relaxation. The chemical nature of the skeleton, which relates it to the mineral kingdom, allows it to hold an energetic record of all that has happened to the body since its beginnings in the mother's womb. So you may gain relevant impressions from this second scan.

2 Note the balance and alignment of the client's body position. You are working on the front of the client's body. Stand at one side of the head. For the purpose of the exercise, assume that you are standing on the client's right side. Hold both palms opposite the top of the skull, about 2–6 inches (5–15 cm) away. With your right palm slowly scan over the top of the skull, over the face, to sense where the spine joins the skull. Bring your left hand to this point. Be aware that you are sensing and moving energy gently forward with your right hand; the left will make available the new energy that is needed.

3 Following the line of the spine, move your right hand down the body to the base of the spine, slowly sensing the energetic happenings in the spine as you go. Keep your left hand at the point where the spine joins the skull. Feel the balance of energy in the spine between your two hands. Bring the left hand down to the base of the spine. Move your right hand gently away from the base out into the aura and follow with the left.

Your action is as follows: move the old energy along the bone structure, using the series of joints as a guide, creating a new state of balance into which new energy flows; move the old energy out of the bone structure into the aura where it will be dealt with at a subtle level.

4 From the mid-line of the spine you now scan the right side of the client's skeleton. Return both hands to the base of the neck where it joins the shoulder girdle, with your right hand able to move toward the right shoulder. Keeping your left hand at the neck, move the right to the shoulder joint. Sense the balance of energy between your two palms. Bring your left hand to the shoulder joint.

5 Move your right hand to the right elbow, follow with the left. Move your right hand to

the wrist, and follow with the left. Move your right hand slowly over the bones of the hand and bring up the left. Move your right hand out into the aura and follow with the left.

6 Move so that you can place both hands over the pelvic girdle where it joins the spine. Keeping your left hand over the center of the pelvis, move your right hand to the client's right hip. Follow with your left hand.

7 Move your right hand to the right knee, then follow with the left. Move your right hand to the ankle and follow with the left. Move your right hand slowly over the bones of the foot, and follow with the left. Move your right hand out into the aura and follow with your left.

8 You are going to move down the left side of the client's skeleton. Move so that you can place both hands over the shoulder girdle where it joins the spine. Move your left hand from the neck to the left shoulder joint. Follow with the right.

9 Move your left hand to the left elbow, then follow with the right. Move your left hand to the wrist and follow with the right. Move your left hand over the bones of the hand, and follow with the right. Move your left hand out into the aura and follow with the right.

10 Move so that you can place both hands over the pelvic girdle where it joins the spine. Move your left hand to the client's left hip. Follow with the right. Move your left hand to the knee, and follow with the right. Move your left hand to the ankle, and follow with the right. Move your left hand over the bones of the left foot and follow with the right. Move your left hand out into the aura and follow with the right.

11 The skeletal scan is completed by checking the balance of the skeletal energy circuits as a whole. Stand opposite the client's feet and hold your palms out about 2–4 inches (5–10 cm) away from them. Your intention is to balance the skeletal circuits. Sense the flow of energies between your palms and the client's soles.

12 Keep your hands in this position until you sense that the two sides of the skeleton are in a state of balance. Move your hands slowly away from the client.

13 Note if there has been any change in body position or alignment.

Returning to Where the System Still Calls for Healing

Now is the time to refer to your intuitive messages as you were carrying out the two healing scans. Do you feel the need to return to a chakra or chakras or somewhere else on the body? Bearing in mind the client's reason for coming for healing, is there somewhere you feel you need to return to? Or is the system still calling for more healing anyway? Position yourself accordingly.

1 Start with the topmost chakra that is calling for more healing. Hold your hands there until you feel all the energetic transactions are completed. Move on to the next chakra (if any). Complete this chakra work by returning to the feet to check the balance of the etheric polarity channels.

2 If you have to work on the body again, do it in a systematic way so that you end with the lowest part of the body. Hold your hands over the place that is calling for healing until you feel that all the energetic transactions have been completed. Complete your work on the body by returning to the feet to check the balance of the body polarity.

You have now carried out the main stages of the healing procedure. It is now time to close the session.

Stand to one side of the client. See her surrounded by the light of protection. This is a sphere of golden light. You can help to create this protection around the client by moving your arms slowly and gently to describe this sphere in the air. This light begins the process of returning the client's chakras to their everyday state so that they begin to close up a little. When you feel that they are completely surrounded by the golden light stand behind the client in the same place as you were when you began the healing procedure.

Give thanks to her at a soul level once more and step up so that you can gently put your hands on her shoulders. This is the signal that the healing procedure has ended. Now stand where she can see you when she opens her eyes. Give the client time to "come back." Speak to her softly, using her name. Help her to return to body consciousness by asking her to become aware of her feet, to wiggle her toes and to rub her legs with her hands. Check her breathing and whether her eyes are focused. These precautions make sure that the client is grounded or returned to earth. This is where our consciousness needs to be when we have to carry out our everyday tasks.

When the client seems ready, help her off the healing couch. Sit together as you did at the start of the session. Again, listen carefully with empathy to any reactions/experiences related to the healing. Remain supportive of what the client wants to do next. If you feel that she needs another healing session suggest this and make another appointment for her to come to see you.

"Stand to one side of the client. See her surrounded by the light of protection. This is a sphere of golden light. You can help create this protection around the client by moving your arms slowly and gently to describe this sphere in the air."

Healing on the Chair

t is not always appropriate or possible for the client to lie on a couch, so it is essential that you also know how to work with a client on a chair. The effects of the work are identical in both cases, but notice the changes in the procedure.

Stand behind the client, a step away from her. Relax and center yourself.

Exercise 20: Healing with the Client on a Chair

You will find it helpful to tape the exercise or to have it read aloud to you.

The Chakra Scan

It is possible to sense the chakras at the back of the body as well as the front. Healing on the chair makes use of this so that your hands will be positioned at the back as well as the front of the body.

Remember that in the learning situation you still need to sense where the chakras are.

1 Make sure the client is comfortable, with a pillow under her feet if necessary. Make sure that there are no crossed limbs and that the client's feet are flat on the floor (or flat on the pillow if the client is using one). Stand in front of the client as you tell her that your signal for beginning the healing procedure will be a light touch on her shoulders. You will also use this same touch to signal that the procedure is over.

2 Stand behind the client, a step away from her. Relax and center yourself. Recall the link between your hands and your heart chakra. Mentally thank the client for this opportunity to work with her and ask that your two souls direct the healing. This continues your

attunement with the client and will help to enable the Healing Triangle.

3 Step up to the client and gently place your hands on her shoulders. You may feel the movement of energy in your hands at this point. Raise your hands up about 2–3 feet (60–90 cm) above the client's crown chakra, about head-width apart, with the palms sloping slightly inward. Gently lower your hands until you feel a resistance from the crown chakra. Stop and allow an interchange of energy. Note in what part of the aura your hands need to be. This is the level (mental or emotional) at which energy is needed. Note also whether energy is leaving your hands or vibrating against them. Lower them a little more if the feeling of resistance allows, but do not touch the crown of the head.

4 Step to one side of the client; for this exercise, stand at the client's right side. As you turn your body, slowly move both your hands opposite the client's brow chakra, with the left hand about a foot away from the back of the head and your right about a foot away from the brow. Be aware that you are gently clearing and sensing as well as making energy available to the brow chakra. Move both your hands slowly in toward the brow chakra until

you feel its energetic resistance. Stop and allow an interchange of energy. Again, note where you are in the client's aura and the sensations in your hands. Move both hands a little farther toward the brow if this is possible. Keep an eye on the state of the client and her breathing.

5 When you feel ready, move both your hands until they are opposite the throat chakra, about a foot away, and proceed as before. You now have data about the relationship between the three chakras. The movements of the scan as described ensure that each chakra comes into balance and that they are in a state of mutual harmony.

6 Move both hands again until they are opposite the heart chakra. Proceed in the same way, being aware and sensitive, with slow and gentle movements. Take time to assess what you are experiencing. You may feel the need to sit on a chair as you move down the system. You should be comfortable too.

7 Move both hands until they are opposite the solar plexus.

8 Move both hands until they are opposite the sacral chakra.

9 Finally move both hands until they are opposite the base chakra. Because of the curvature of the body, to sense the base chakra, hold your left hand above the client's groin with the right under the base of the spine. Your two hands make an angle of about 45 degrees.

10 When your work on the base chakra feels complete, slowly move your hands to the client's feet. You are going to assess the state of balance of the two complementary subtle-energy streams. Recall Exercise 5, "Checking Polarity Balance." Hold your palms about 6–12 inches (15–30 cm) away from the client's feet. Sense the flow of energies between your hands and the chakras of the client's feet. Keep your hands in this position until you sense that the energy flow is in balance.

11 You may find it more comfortable to assess the balance of the body via the shoulders. This is just as effective. Simply hold your palms about 6–12 inches (15–30 cm) away from the client's shoulders and work with the energy balancing in the same way.

This completes the chakra healing scan. You now have a diagnostic picture of the client at a subtle-energetic level. This is your perception and should not be conveyed to the client. How does it relate to the client's story and to any impressions that you may have received?

Recall that the chakras impact on the physical body through the endocrine glands and from there to the various organs and tissues. In this way, the chakra scan also works with the organs and tissues of the body.

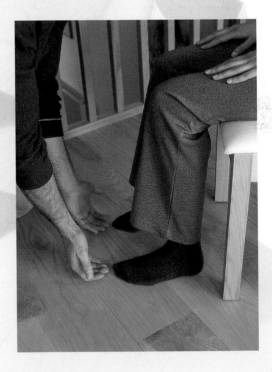

The Skeletal Scan

1 For the skeletal healing scan return to your position standing behind the client. Recall the illustration of the skeleton and its energy circuits on page 37. Your intention is to work with these circuits and with the skeletal system. Check that your client is still relaxed and breathing normally. If she has gone to sleep this is fine, do not wake her. She will not fall out of the chair! Check your own relaxation. The chemical nature of the skeleton, which relates it to the mineral kingdom, allows it to hold an energetic record of all that has happened to the body since its beginnings in the mother's womb. So you may gain relevant impressions from this second scan.

2 Note the balance and alignment of the client's body position. Hold both palms opposite the top of the skull about 2–6 inches (5–15 cm) away with the left palm uppermost. With the right hand, slowly scan over the top and back of the skull to sense where the spine joins the skull. Bring your left hand to this point. Be aware that you are clearing and sensing with your right hand, while the left makes new energy available.

3 Following the line of the spine, move your right hand to the base of the spine, slowly sensing the energetic happenings in the spine as you go. Keep your left hand at the point where the spine joins the skull. Now cup your two hands to feel the balance of energy in the whole spine. Bring the left hand down to the base of the spine. Move your right hand gently away from the base out into the aura and follow with the left.

Your action is as follows: move the old energy along the bone structure, using the series of joints as a guide, creating a new state of balance into which new energy flows; move the old energy out of the bone structure into the aura where it will be dealt with at a subtle level.

4 Stand to one side of the client. For the purpose of the exercise, we will assume that you are standing on the client's right side. From the mid-line of the spine you now scan the right side of the client's skeleton. Return both hands to the base of the neck where it joins the back of the shoulder girdle, with your right hand able to move toward the right shoulder. Keeping your left hand at the neck, move the right to the shoulder joint. Sense the balance of energy between your two palms. Bring your left hand to the shoulder joint.

5 Move your right hand to the right elbow, then follow with the left. Move your right hand to the wrist and follow with the left. Move your right hand slowly over the bones of the hand, and follow with the left. Move your right hand out into the aura and follow with the left.

6 Move so that you can place both hands over the back of the pelvic girdle where it joins the spine. Keeping your left hand over the center of the pelvis, move your right hand to the client's right hip. Follow with your left hand.

7 Move your right hand to the right knee, follow with the left. Move your right hand to the ankle, and follow with the left. Move your right hand slowly over the bones of the foot, and follow with the left. Move your right hand out into the aura and follow with your left.

8 Move so that you can place both hands over the back of the shoulder girdle where it joins the spine. You are going to move down the left side of the client's skeleton. Move your left hand from the back of the neck to the left shoulder joint. Follow with the right.

9 Move your left hand to the left elbow, then follow with the right. Move your left hand to the wrist, then follow with the right. Move your left hand over the bones of the hand, and follow with the right. Move your left hand out into the aura and follow with the right.

10 Move into a position from which you can place both hands over the back of the pelvic girdle where it joins the spine. Move your left hand to the client's left hip and then follow with the right. Move your left hand to the knee, and follow with the right. Move your left hand to the ankle and follow with the right. Move your left hand over the bones of the left foot, and bring up the right. Move your left hand out into the aura and follow up with the right.

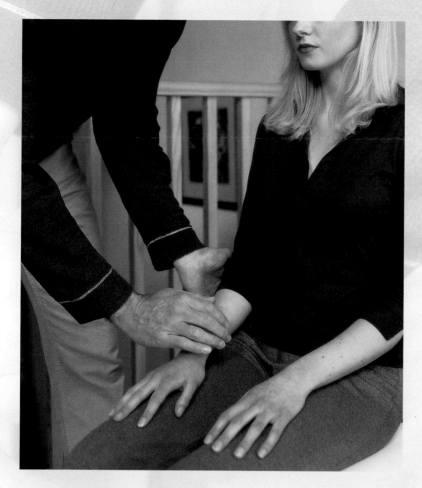

11 The skeletal scan is completed by checking the balance of the skeletal energy circuits as a whole. Hold your palms over the client's feet about 2–4 inches (5–10 cm) away from them. Your intention is to balance the skeletal circuits. Sense the flow of energies between your palms and the client's feet.

12 Keep your hands in this position until you sense that the two sides of the

skeleton are in a state of balance. Move your hands slowly away from the client. As before, it is just as effective to work with the polarity balance of the body via the shoulders. Hold your palms above the client's shoulders, about 2–4 inches (5–10 cm) away from them, and work with the energy balancing in the same way.

13 Note if there has been any change in body position or alignment.

Returning to Where the System Still Calls for Healing

Now is the time to refer to your intuitive messages as you were carrying out the two healing scans. Do you feel the need to return to a chakra or chakras or somewhere else on the body? Bearing in mind the client's reason for coming for healing, is there somewhere you feel you need return to? Or is the system still calling for more healing anyway? Position yourself accordingly

1 Start with the topmost chakra that is calling for more healing. Hold your hands there until you feel all the energetic transactions are completed. Move on to the next chakra (if any). Complete this chakra work by rechecking the balance of the etheric polarity channels.

2 If you have to work on the body again, do it in a systematic way so that you end with the lowest part of the body. Hold your hands over the place that is calling for healing until you feel that all the energetic transactions have been completed. Complete your work on the body by rechecking the balance of the body polarity.

You have now carried out the main stages of the healing procedure. It is time to close the session.

Stand behind the client, about a step away from the chair. See the client surrounded by the light of protection. This is a sphere of golden light. You can help create this protection around the client by moving your arms slowly and gently to describe this sphere in the air. This light begins the process of returning the client's chakras to their everyday state so that they begin to close up a little.

When you feel that the client is completely surrounded by the golden light, give thanks to her at a soul level once more and step up so that you can gently put your hands on her shoulders. This is the signal that the healing procedure has ended. In a soft voice call her name and repeat that the healing is completed. Now stand where she can see you when she opens her eyes. Give her time to "come back." Help her return to body consciousness by asking her to become aware of her feet, to wiggle her toes, and to rub her legs with her hands. Check the client's breathing and whether her eyes are focused. These precautions make sure that the client is grounded or returned to earth. This is where our consciousness needs to be when we have to carry out our everyday tasks.

When she seems ready, help the client to stand up and move away from the healing chair. Sit together opposite each other as you did at the start of the session. Again, listen carefully with empathy to her reactions to the healing. Remain supportive of what the client wants to do next. If you feel that she needs another healing session suggest this and make another appointment as necessary.

Clearing
and Closing Down

Once the client has left, clear your hands by visualizing light washing over them. Do the same with the furniture in the healing room. This ensures that no energies from one client will interfere with the work you need to do with the next. If you intuitively feel that the room itself needs clearing, carry out the procedures described in "Attuning the Healing Space" (pages 62–63).

These procedures also help you to break the link mentally between yourself and the client so that you will be able to empathize with a new person and approach her with a clear mind.

When you have reached the end of the working day, you need to relax and bring your energy systems back to everyday functioning. For example, your whole energy field has opened up to the flow of healing energy and to the energies of your clients. This includes the chakras. If you increase your sensitivity in any way, especially by working as a spiritual healer, then you have to take responsibility for your own energetic health.

Except for the energy needed to concentrate and to stand up to work, your overall energy level is not usually depleted when working as a healer. If you do feel depleted then it may well be a sign that you need to look carefully at how you operate. But any person with a high level of sensitivity can be drained of energy in places where there are low levels of energy, such as supermarkets, shopping malls, and any area covered with concrete.

One of your main tools of protection and maintenance is the closing down procedure.

This means clearing and balancing your energy field, regulating your chakra system, and creating a sphere of protection around yourself.

Begin your closing down by carrying out Exercise 15, "Clearing the Energy Field." Stand under the silver shower and let it relax and cleanse you.

Then reduce the activity of your chakras with the next exercises (pages 86-87).

Exercise 21:
Regulating the Chakras

Practice this exercise as part of your closing-down procedure or any time you intuitively feel that you need to bring your chakras back to everyday functioning. For the purpose of the exercise you can visualize the chakras as flowers with their petals wide open. The chakras are regulated by closing the petals a little. On no account should they be completely closed. The idea is to regulate activity, not to stop the chakras from functioning altogether. It may be helpful to have this exercise read aloud to you.

1 Stand with your feet about shoulder-width apart. Relax and breathe normally. Recall the balanced colors of the chakras. Put your mind in your crown center and see the violet flower with its open petals. Allow them to close up a little.

2 Let your mind move to the brow. See the indigo/royal blue flower close up a little.

3 Move to the throat chakra. See the sky blue flower close up a little.

4 Move to the heart chakra in the center of your chest. See the green flower close up a little.

5 Move to the solar plexus chakra below the ribcage. See the golden yellow flower close up a little.

6 Move to the sacral chakra, just below the navel. See the orange flower close up a little.

7 Move to the base chakra. See the red flower close up a little.

8 Now see a sphere of colored light around you. The first color that comes to mind is the color of light that you need to keep the balance of your system in place.

This exercise should always be followed by the third part of your closing-down procedure, which is the next exercise.

Exercise 22:
The Sphere of Protection

Use this exercise at the end of your closing-down procedure, at the end of the day, or any time you feel the need for energetic protection. Golden light, linked to your intention, provides a protective shield that allows positive energies into your field but keeps out negative energies.

1 Stand as you were in the previous exercise, relaxed and breathing normally. Imagine that you can surround yourself with a sphere of light by using the breath, just as you did in Exercise 10, "The Rainbow Breath"(page 43).

2 As you breathe in, visualize golden light spreading from under your feet up the front of your body. As you exhale, see the light extending down your back until you are totally enclosed in a sphere of golden light. Use more than one breath if you need to.

3 If this exercise follows Exercise 21, "Regulating the Chakras"(see page 86), see the sphere of golden light surrounding the sphere of color that is maintaining the balance of your chakras.

Keeping Records

As I suggested at the beginning of the book, you will find it invaluable to keep a record, such as a journal, of what you do. This becomes imperative once you start working as a healer. You should keep a simple record of what each person came for, the treatment you gave, possible reactions and nonmedical assessments, and any notes you need to add on those points. Bear in mind that clients are allowed access to these records and that the records may be protected by privacy legislation.

Exploring
Spiritual Healing

In 1987, Professor William A. Tiller of Stanford University was making a case for the serious investigation of the etheric and the development of a science of the etheric to balance the present science of the material (see his Foreword to Richard Gerber's *Vibrational Medicine*). Not long after the publication of Dr. Gerber's book, the International Society for the Study of Subtle Energies and Energy Medicine (ISSSEEM) was formed in the United States to support study and increase dialog among clinicians, healers, and the scientific and medical communities.

Spiritual healing is subtle-energy medicine with a soul or spiritual base. In other words, its methodology arises from the premise that all energy has a spiritual origin, all energy is spirit. By working through and with the subtle-energy system, and with the flow of these energies, spiritual healing is the only complementary therapy that is developing a science of the etheric.

As a way of exploring the new science of the etheric, this chapter looks at the range of applications of spiritual healing, beginning with oneself then moving out into the family. This includes the role of healing in life issues such as birth, terminal illness, and death.

From here we look at how we can offer a special kind of help to the local, and ultimately, the global environment. So often, when we are faced with news of illness, accident, or disaster, we feel powerless. It may be on the television screen, thousands of miles away, yet we are disturbed because the images are in our own home. We are involved by just seeing and hearing them, but there seems nothing we can do. Yet, because of Oneness, we feel the impulse to do something. The various forms of distant healing described in this chapter offer ways in which we can be of service through positive action.

Self Healing

Working with your own health means empowering yourself by taking responsibility for it. Although it is obviously the role of any therapy to relieve suffering, most conditions are easier to bear when people feel that they can play their part in treatment and management. The best way for healers to learn about taking responsibility is to realize that they can work on themselves as well as others.

The body is our friend, so its information about our state of harmony should be heeded rather than rejected or treated as a nuisance. We tend to get upset about body information we receive when it comes in the form of distress, pain, or the symptoms of a condition. Before we reach this state, we can start creating a lifestyle that promotes balance and harmony.

"The body is our friend, so its information about our state of harmony should be heeded rather than rejected or treated as a nuisance."

Many of the exercises you have practiced so far will help you to do this, and some you will need to do on a regular basis, such as good breathing and relaxation.

But no matter how many precautions we may take, healers still have to deal with life and what it brings, like everyone else. This is where self-healing comes in. You can begin by taking an inventory of how you assess your physical, emotional, and mental levels.

Exercise 23:
Assessment for Self-Healing

Have some note-making materials available.

1 Sit comfortably, relax, and breathe normally. Imagine that you can be an impartial observer of yourself. If necessary, in your mind's eye, step away from yourself in order to do this. But you are a loving, not a judgmental or critical observer.

2 As you survey the body in front of you, what do you think of it and what comes immediately to mind? What do you feel about its state of balance and what seems to put it out of balance? What parts of you seem to be out of harmony with the rest and why is this? Give yourself time to listen to your body's responses rather than your mind's, and thank your body for its cooperation. Now make some notes about your experience.

3 Check your relaxation. Again, as an impartial observer of this person you think of as you, look at your emotions. How balanced are they? Are there emotions you never feel or do not allow yourself to feel? Are there emotions you do not feel in control of, or maybe they control you sometimes? Can you have fun? Listen to the response and notice what your mind wants to do with the response. Now make a note of your experience.

4 Check your relaxation again and watch what your body does when your mind goes to work. Note also how you feel. Look at your mindset. What makes you anxious? What makes you fearful? What makes you close up? Whom do you dislike and what do you dislike about that person? Do you find it easy to be wholehearted, openhearted, courageous, passionate? Are your beliefs about other people and the world your own or what you have received from others? Once again, make a note of your experience.

You will probably need to break this exercise up into parts to get a true assessment. As you read through your notes and recall your experiences with the questions, you get a picture of yourself. Any surprises? Doing the exercise as truthfully as you can is an act of courage. Congratulate yourself; you are going to need courage like this as you develop your healing skills and a healing heart.

Having completed your inventory you should have an idea of what requires healing. Let's follow with some self-healing exercises to bring the harmony you need.

Exercise 24:
Using the Breath in Self-Healing:
The Body

You may find it helpful to tape the exercise or have a partner read it to you.

1 Carry out the complete personal attunement process that is described in Chapter 3 (see pages 60–63) as if you were going to work with a client. Make sure that you ask for protection and that you feel safe and protected before you proceed.

2 Sit comfortably with your feet flat on the floor with no crossed limbs or lie comfortably on a couch. Relax and take three or four full breaths to clear the lungs. Let go with the out-breaths.

3 Now imagine that you can breathe the breath of life into your heart center. As you inhale, your heart center is filled with light. With the next breath, as you exhale send the light of the heart to the top of your head and then down your spine. The light relaxes every part it touches. Inhale and send the light down your left arm, from the shoulder to the tips of the fingers. Inhale and send the light down the right arm. Inhale and send the light down the left leg, from the hip to the ends of the toes. Inhale and send the light down the right leg. Inhale and send the light down the front of your body. Inhale and send the light down the back of your body.

4 Use the same heart breath to send light to any place in your body that is calling for healing. Each time breathe slowly and gently without straining. You may feel the need to hold your hands over the place to reinforce the work. You can be confident that the directed light from the heart center activates the body's healing processes.

Exercise 25:
Using the Breath in Self-Healing: Mind and Emotions

This exercise extends the same self-healing technique to the mental and emotional levels. Take time to identify what you feel needs healing. Unannounced material may surface and have to be dealt with. This will occur because this is the right time for this to happen. In both exercises, using your hands where you feel the need will reinforce the focusing of the energy.

1 Check your attunement. Assume the same position as in the previous exercise. Relax and take slow and gentle full breaths, letting go with the out-breath until your whole body has become relaxed.

2 In this relaxed state try to identify where in your body you feel your emotional distress or feelings of being upset. Allow your body to help you. It may be more than one place. Or you may well feel that the location is at a subtle level in a chakra (especially the solar plexus) or in your energy field.

3 Now imagine that you can breathe the breath of life into your heart center. As you inhale, your heart center is filled with light. Once you have established your light center, you can then use the healing breath to heal your emotional distress.

4 Use the heart breath to send light to those places in your body, in a chakra or in the aura, that are calling for emotional healing. Let go of the distress with the out-breath. Each time breathe slowly and gently without straining, letting go of the emotional energies with the out- breath.

5 To heal mental distress, anxieties, turmoil, etc., proceed in the same way. Check your attunement. In the relaxed state try to identify where in your body you feel your mental distress, disturbing thoughts, etc. Allow your body to help you. It may be more than one place. Or you may well feel that the location is at a subtle level in a chakra (especially the solar plexus) or in your energy field.

6 Once again imagine that you can breathe the breath of life into your heart center. As you inhale, your heart center is filled with light. With your light center established this time, use the healing breath to heal your mental distress.

7 Use the heart breath to send light to those places in your body, in a chakra or in the aura, that are calling for mental healing. Let go of the distress with the out-breath. Each time breathe slowly and gently without straining, letting go of the mental energies with the out-breath.

Healing and New Life

As I mentioned in the "Soul Journey" (see pages 14-15), we, as souls, choose to come to planet earth for our own unique reasons. These will include particular experiences and expressions through these experiences. For some of us our decision to come to earth may also arise from the law of cause and effect (also known as karma). This happens when soul decides to address imbalances caused by a person's actions in a previous life. The reincarnating soul contains a record of all its past experiences.

The totality of all the different reasons for being born form soul's mission. The soul chooses to align the birth with as many factors as possible to ensure that the mission will be accomplished. So we choose our mother and father, the time and place of birth, our name (which carries a specific vibration that may affect the life path), and the

As far as spiritual healing is concerned, at the heart of this great journey of soul is the fact that we are all one and that we are Oneness. This means that we are not in a position to pass judgment on the lives of others no matter what we feel about them. To function as healers, as transmitters of unconditional love, we have to be able to stand back from our ego perceptions and see the world from a divine perspective.

We all choose our parents and the time and place of our birth.

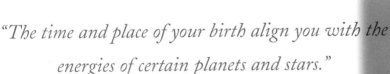

"The time and place of your birth align you with the energies of certain planets and stars."

spiritual environment in which we will find ourselves. We also decide our basic health patterns and whether our lives will be learning experiences for others as well as ourselves.

The time and place of your birth align you with the energies of certain planets and stars. They may also decide your race, religion, and the historical setting for your life.

Souls choose whether they wish to experience being in the womb, the trauma of birth, and life after birth. Many souls do not become embodied until the moment of birth, or just after. As soon as this takes place, the little person begins the task of expressing soul. The soul knows how much this task may be enhanced or thwarted by the inherited genetic makeup and the mental conditioning that the person will encounter.

Healing, Pregnancy, and Birth

During the process of incarnation, soul is in touch with the mother and father and later, following conception, the growing embryo. It is very beneficial for the mother to have healing during pregnancy. She may be experiencing a number of stresses that are disrupting harmony on more than one level. These can be addressed during the session. The fetus also enjoys the benefit of restoring harmony.

Pregnant women are frequently aware of another soul around them and healing puts them in touch with the qualities of the being to whom they will give birth. In some countries, a healer is allowed to be present at the hospital at the time of birth as long as the birth is supervised by the midwife and/or doctor and the healer is not there for financial gain.

The Experience of a Baby or a Young Child

During the early weeks of life, the baby spends much of its time sleeping. This allows it to move its consciousness out of the body and stay in contact with the Source. It also lessens the traumatic impact of leaving the warmth and comfort of the womb to become dependent on others for all its needs. But soul has come to live an earthly life and it must begin to function through the body consciousness. The baby soon develops a personality of its own, and by about three years of age the increasing demands of the growing physical person begin to overshadow its spiritual reality.

Working with Children and Young People

Children are very open to healing energies. Up to the age of about three they still have a conscious link with Oneness, so that rebalancing happens very quickly.

There are circumstances, however, when children carry within their consciousness traces of birth trauma or negative womb experiences. This can happen, for example, when they have been exposed to the mother's or parents' emotional, mental, or physical distress. The child cannot verbalize this but it will reveal itself during the healing.

In rare cases children have pre-existence awareness that may manifest as distress about being in a physical body. In such cases the baby may be

"When a child is brought for healing, the procedures are the same as with an adult."

physically well but refuses to be placated and does not respond to the love shown to it. Healing is able to help these babies, and their parents, by calming them and linking them to the soul that brought about their birth.

Sometimes the incoming being finds the restrictions of its little body too great, and it experiences great feelings of frustration and limitation. Again, healing can link consciousness to soul's mission and calm the child.

Rudolf Steiner (1861–1925), a pioneer in the spiritual development of children, noticed how the chakras were beneficially stimulated through some of the so-called childhood illnesses. The soul finds many ways to trigger the awakening of the chakras, and this is often confirmed when children are brought for healing.

The language of soul comes to us through the subtle-energy system and the chakras, so the child soon manifests any imbalance in its life. The child's body is quick to show its parents and the world what is happening. The aware parent also sees how the child makes visible any disharmony on the emotional and mental levels.

To avoid ill-health and mental and emotional stress we all need to remember that we are soul and why we are here.

As children grow into young adults they pass through a number of important transitions that may be stressful for them. Around the ages of three and four the open link with the Source begins to close down and the child needs to be held within the family. But at this age they may spend time outside the home at nursery school. If parents take time to be with their children they will notice that each child has its own unique patterns of growth and maturity and that each soul has a way of signaling how well the child is coping with the changes.

Healing and Child Development

When a child is brought for healing, the procedures are the same as with an adult. Children should not be talked down to, but respect should be shown to the soul in the child body.

The legal position is that the child must have already seen a doctor, and the healer must obtain signed parental permission to work with any child below the age of consent. The parent or guardian should also be present during the healing session. If working with children is calling to you, you will need to have an understanding of child development and the particular problems that children and their parents encounter. Working with damaged or traumatized children is a specialized field and healers should make sure that they are competent to handle this responsibility in a totally professional way.

As we plunge deeper and deeper into physical life we may lose sight of the fact that we are soul and why we came here. For many, disconnection from soul and the sacred can become a prime cause of ill-health as the body tries to awaken us to the situation. Not knowing why we are here may also be a cause for mental and emotional stress.

The soul, however, never loses contact with us. It speaks to us through the language of feeling. Our urge to express ourselves and do something special in life are soul's whispers about our reality. No wonder we are disappointed when we feel we have talents we do not use. Sights, sounds, and smells may suddenly resonate deep inside like memories of something we thought we had forgotten. These are soul's ways of trying to get through to our personality (ego), to help us remember who we really are.

With maturity, the process of recall may seem incredibly difficult. We find that we now have to deal with other people's versions of who we are, who we ought to be, how we ought to behave, perhaps even what we ought to do in life. A healer may be asked to help in this unraveling process and needs to know about the many influences on the person when he or she was growing up. Our response to what happens to us has a great bearing on how we develop and the kind of person we become. Our way of responding is also formed by the influences around us as we grow toward maturity.

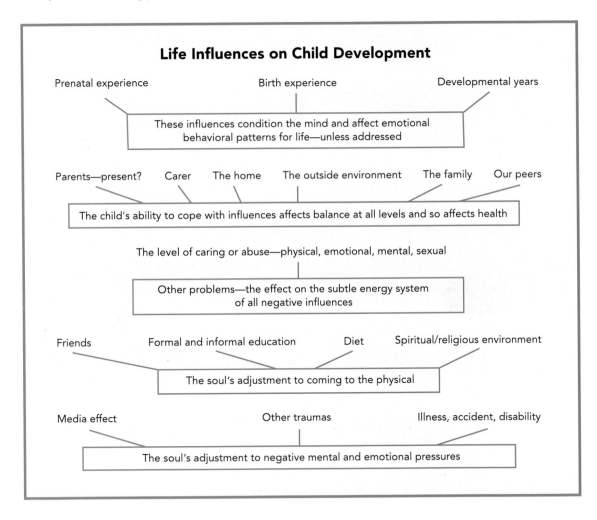

Life Influences on Child Development

Prenatal experience   Birth experience   Developmental years

These influences condition the mind and affect emotional behavioral patterns for life—unless addressed

Parents—present?   Carer   The home   The outside environment   The family   Our peers

The child's ability to cope with influences affects balance at all levels and so affects health

The level of caring or abuse—physical, emotional, mental, sexual

Other problems—the effect on the subtle energy system of all negative influences

Friends   Formal and informal education   Diet   Spiritual/religious environment

The soul's adjustment to coming to the physical

Media effect   Other traumas   Illness, accident, disability

The soul's adjustment to negative mental and emotional pressures

"Spiritual healing also considers the soul influence on our development as individuals."

The Soul's Influences on Child Development

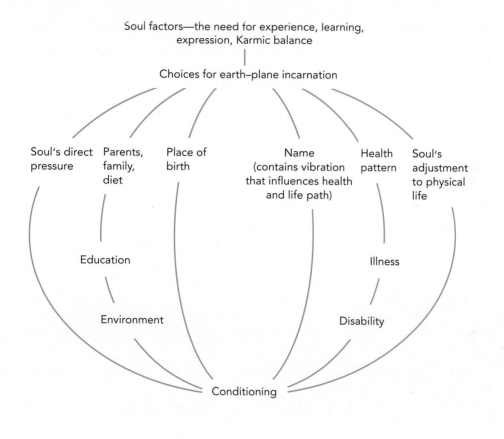

Soul factors—the need for experience, learning, expression, Karmic balance

Choices for earth–plane incarnation

Soul's direct pressure

Parents, family, diet

Place of birth

Name (contains vibration that influences health and life path)

Health pattern

Soul's adjustment to physical life

Education

Illness

Environment

Disability

Conditioning

Personality factors will determine levels of experience, learning, expression, and karmic balance though each individual's personal balance

"Though our personal balance may be influenced by all of the above factors, we find true balance when we align the needs of our personality with the soul and the soul mission."

Animals and Healing

All beings are spirit—energy patterns that emanate from the Source/Oneness. Just like ourselves, they exist as soul and have the communication level of the etheric. There is no animal, therefore, however small, that is not open to and does not respond to healing. The whole area of spiritual healing with all types of animals—not just pets, horses, and other domesticated animals—is waiting to be explored.

For animals, group consciousness is more evident than selfconsciousness because of their different role in creation. But as animals become domesticated they develop degrees of self-consciousness that are most noticeable in pets. Most groups of animals have different means of communication and expression that in most groups we are hardly beginning to understand even when we are actually aware of them. At present, both the giant octopus and the dolphin are considered very intelligent because scientists are able to interpret some of the ways they operate. The lives of millions of other species still amaze us because we know what they do but do not understand the how or the why of their behavior.

"Their lack of selfconsciousness makes most animals, like children, very open to the energies of healing."

These are the findings of modern material science. Indigenous scientific studies have looked at many animals holistically, in the same manner that spiritual healing would use—viewing animals as multidimensional beings within a multidimensional

*We become very attached
to our pets, reflecting a primeval
sacred link between human beings
and the animal kingdom.*

landscape. The findings of indigenous science give us a deeper knowledge and understanding of animals and their world.

Once we move away from the level of the physical, the role of animals is truly awesome and exciting. Each animal is engendered with areas of power and wisdom that it shares with all other beings. Indigenous peoples, such as Native Americans and Australian Aboriginals, to name a few, have known this and made use of it in their everyday lives and their approach to the sacred. In the so-called developed world people have been largely unable to do this because we are unaware and therefore do not share these beliefs. Yet the evidence of our ancestors, such as the art of the Celtic peoples, suggests that maybe we once had a greater kinship with the earth family.

There is obvious scope for a biological and zoological science of the etheric that could begin by assessing the data amassed by those cultures that have approached the animal kingdom with respect for its sacred nature. Many pet owners experience remarkable bonds with animals that encompass a range of communications. It is not surprising that the death of a pet can be as heartbreaking as the death of a relative or close friend.

Their lack of selfconsciousness makes most animals, like children, very open to the energies of healing. If you feel the call to work with animals then look at the extra training that you might need. A sick animal should first be taken to a veterinarian. Most veterinarians do not object to spiritual healing being given to the animals in their care and many can

testify to its effectiveness. Remember that healing is a complementary therapy and that healers do not countermand veterinary treatment any more than they would countermand the medical treatment of a human being.

Mammals have a chakra system very similar to that of humans, though their functions do not include the same life issues. They can be sensed in just the same way as you learned in Exercises 3 and 4, "Locating the Major Chakras" (pages 26–27). A subtle-energy system is present in all animals but becomes less like the human system as the animal form moves farther away from the mammalian pattern.

As you start to work with any animal, check your attunement in the usual way; allow soul to direct the healing and see where your hands want to go. Be sure to keep a record of everything you do.

Working with Plants and the Environment

Planet earth is a being in its own right with an etheric and soul level. It provides support for the earth family of plants and animals (which includes us humans). The earth generates its own energies, conveying them to the earth family. The earth is also sustained in its present form by energies from the sun and the cosmos.

Sustainability depends on energetic balance and harmony throughout all the systems. Humans are just a part of this whole but we have it in our power to upset the energetic balance of every other life form and the planetary environment on which all life forms depend. To date, technologically advanced humans have ignored the interdependent aspect of life, and the planet is now in a precarious state of imbalance. As a result millions of life forms have decided to leave for good (become extinct).

The earth is a being with its own soul journey and its own mission. Just like our own bodies, it will do what it can to alert us to the situation and, if necessary, take action to restore energetic balance.

Working with the Landscape

There is much that spiritual healers can do to help besides looking at their own lifestyles. There is landscape where you live. This may be in the country, where landscape is easily identifiable, or in the city, where it is not so obvious. Pause for a moment and realize that wherever you live you are on the earth. Concrete, asphalt, and buildings have all been supplied by the earth and have generally been obtained without gratitude or consideration.

If you activate your hands, either by the mental intention or as in the very first exercise (page 18), you will soon sense whether healing is needed where you live, where you travel to, or where you work. Rest assured that every act of healing, which is an offering of love from you to the planet, brings back the Light that is desperately needed. The presence of the Light may heal direct damage as well as encourage further positive changes.

The countryside needs your help too. Any modification to the landscape is a cause for healing. House- and road-building break up the living areas of countless beings, and materials are brought in from distant places as a new environment is created. Energy lines and patterns are disturbed and destroyed. Farming practices may also be an exploitation of the land rather than a cooperation with it, creating new healing needs. As an aware healer you may find this area of work is calling to you.

Working with Plants

The changes mentioned above usually involve the plant world too. Plants respond readily to healing. Trees and other plants are frequently involved in felling and pruning. You will notice a change in your garden when you help the plant world to recover from such horticultural practices. Working with a plant in the home is a good place to find out about how plants respond to healing or simply your loving concern about them.

Use a potted plant that shows signs of stress.

Exercise 26:
Rebalancing the Energy Field of a Plant

1 Relax and take a few full breaths. Focus on your heart chakra and attune yourself. Just as if the plant were a client, communicate to the plant that you wish to help it. Take time to listen to any response that the plant may give. This may be like a voice or sensation in your heart center or another chakra. You need to be open to the possibility of nonverbal communication.

2 If it seems appropriate, hold your hands near the plant with the palms directed toward it. Move your hands toward the plant until they are aware of the plant's energies. Then see if you are aware of the plant in any other way. Allow energy to leave your hands to be absorbed by the plant. Keep your hands in this position until the energy transaction is complete.

3 Make a note of the day and time and, if you can find out, the position of the moon's phase (a diary usually provides this information). Build a database of your work with individual or groups of plants. Decide if you can draw any conclusions about how to work with plants in the future. Your conclusions will help you to decide how effective it would be for you to extend your healing to plants outside the home, in parks and gardens and farther to wild areas.

Extending Your Healing Sensitivity

Sensing a Mental Condition

The mind is the instrument of soul and its role is to enable us to be conscious of experience. It is there to serve. The mind has three main components: thought, intelligence, and will. Intelligence gives us the power to choose, and the will is the force that we can put behind our choices. The brain is the physical processor of these mental activities. The brain also tells mind what is happening to us, which leads to new mental activities.

Because the mind is designed to serve, it is conditioned by experience. The brain is able to store memories, which in turn affect the mind. This is where our responses to life experience begin to condition how we think, feel, and act. We develop patterns of thinking, based on our experiences, that influence how we act in any given situation.

Problems come when our patterns of thinking do not serve us, preventing us from functioning as we would like to and achieving our goals. We can still exercise choice, but our choices are now based on our conditioning. This is the basis of judgment and prejudice. It is difficult for us to accept that we are seeing the world and everything in it through the distorting lens of our mindsets. When we are made aware of this in some way, it tends to register within us as mental distress.

Through the transmission of energies within the subtle system, we may register mental distress on the emotional level and also feel it in the body. The body may go further to create a physical condition as a signal that something is out of balance. Every choice we make registers as an energetic

Our brains enable us to learn new activities and store the information so that we can carry them out again in the future.

"It is better to say 'I'm suffering' than to say 'This landscape is ugly.'"

Simone Weil, philosopher and mystic (1909–1943)

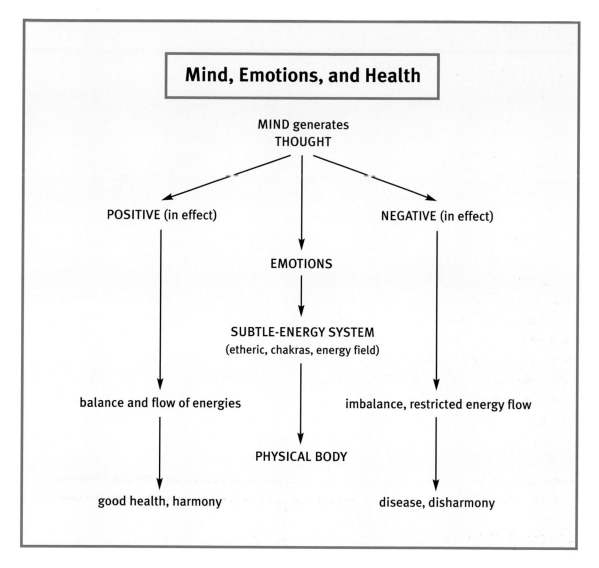

Mind, Emotions, and Health

MIND generates
THOUGHT

POSITIVE (in effect)　　　　　　　　NEGATIVE (in effect)

EMOTIONS

SUBTLE-ENERGY SYSTEM
(etheric, chakras, energy field)

balance and flow of energies　　　　imbalance, restricted energy flow

PHYSICAL BODY

good health, harmony　　　　　　disease, disharmony

event and has a corresponding effect. In the third part of the healing procedure you return to where healing is still called for. If it did not manifest during the chakra scan, this is when a mental condition will be detected in the aura at the level of the mental zone as an energetic resistance, layer, or area. Work with this effect in the usual way until you feel that the energy transaction is completed.

We have been considering everyday levels of mental distress or depression. It should be emphasized, however, that when a client is being treated for a mental condition, healers should seek information about any medication the client may be on, ask for details of the medical practitioner supervising the treatment, and make sure they have a referral source for information and advice.

Without the relevant professional training, healers should always refer clients to someone who is competent to deal with such cases. You are not rejecting them because you can offer to send them distant healing while keeping in touch with them (see "Distant Healing" on page 114).

Sensing an Emotional Condition

Another important field of work is the healing of emotional conditions. Emotions are generated when mind interacts with physical experience. When we are functioning in a healthy way, emotions tell us how much we like or dislike the experience. This is a problem only when experiences have negative outcomes for us.

Soul uses feelings to communicate with us. When we listen to our feelings they indicate which experiences are good for us and which are not. But mental conditioning may prevent us from making the best decision for ourselves. Our emotions are triggered again to tell us how much we like the results of our choices.

People may come for healing without discussing their emotional state. This may be their reaction to the presenting condition. But during the chakra scan or your stage three work, the emotional disturbance will show itself by the position of your hands in the client's aura.

You need to be quite confident that you are able to handle a range of emotional situations and, if not you should refer your client on. Where a client has indicated that she would like you to work with a particular emotional condition such as bereavement, for example, carry out the healing procedure and, with the client's consent, complete the session using a modification of Exercise 6, "Sensing Color in the Major Chakras" (see page 31). The exercise can be used to empower the client to sense how her feelings are manifesting in the subtle-energy system and how she can help herself energetically.

Exercise 27: Working with Color to Balance the Chakras

Before starting, you should be proficient in practicing Exercise 6, "Sensing Color in the Major Chakras" with a partner. Go through this new exercise with a partner until you feel confident to use it with a client. For the purpose of the exercise your partner is called the "client" and you will be standing at her right side. Have a chair nearby if you need it when working with the lower chakras. You are going to help the client to be aware of the energies of her chakras. The second part of the exercise empowers the person to make energetic changes.

1 The client should sit in the healing chair with feet flat on the floor and hands resting palms-down on the thighs. (The palms-down position allows a person to be more aware of internal processes.) She should be relaxed and breathing normally.

2 Stand to one side of the client. Hold your left palm about 4 inches (10 cm) away from the back of the client's throat chakra. Hold your right palm about 3 feet (1 meter) away from the client's crown chakra. Ask her to focus on the area of the crown of the head to look at her inner screen with relaxed vision and describe what she sees. At the same time bring your right hand slowly in toward the crown chakra.

Stop as soon as you feel the energetic resistance of the chakra and note where your hand is in the field (aura). You should find a corroboration between where you have stopped and the client's description as the "screen" comes into focus.

3 Make a mental note of the color and any other descriptions such as darkness, lightness, dots, an uneven edge to the picture, etc. These are all ways in which the client perceives her mental or emotional state as it is registered in the chakra.

4 Ask the client how she feels as she looks at the screen. Does anything come to mind? Make a mental note about these reactions also. You may sense some energetic activity, including healing, going on. Allow these transactions to take place in a confident and relaxed manner before moving to the next chakra. Your own comments should not form part of the exercise.

5 Carefully work your way together through the system until you both have data about every chakra. Let the client rest for a few moments without leaving the healing field that has been created.

6 Return to the crown chakra position. Explain its color of energetic balance. Ask the client to clear her inner screen mentally and to flood it with a vibrant color violet. How difficult is it for her to do this? How does she feel as she sees this new color?

7 Proceed in this way through the chakras, stating the color of balance. Once the client has reached the base and restored a vibrant color red, teach her how to surround herself with the sphere of protection. Ask her to use the breath to create the sphere of golden light (see Exercise 22, "The Sphere of Protection", page 87).

8 Find out if the client has any further comments to make about the exercise. Your own comments should not be offered to the client, nor should you discuss any energetic diagnosis you have formed. This would be poor professional healing, and would also undermine the empowering function of the work.

"She saw orange in her throat and blue in her sacral chakra.

The balance colors were reversed."

The previous exercise presents the healer with a range of energetic data that, along with the client's story, provides a very useful diagnostic record of her mental and/or emotional state (conditions of balance and harmony within the subtle energy system).

Consider the following examples: A bereaved person described the color in his base chakra as "a dirty brown." The heart color green had descended to the base and merged with red. The person was so devastated by losing a cherished loved one that his survival was threatened. His feelings that life was no longer worth living produced the sense of "dirtiness" in the chakras. He had, however, come for healing, and the descent of the heart seemed to point to a cry for help coming from this center of his love.

A writer came for healing as a last attempt to cure writer's block. She saw orange in her throat and blue in her sacral chakra. The balance colors were reversed. In her efforts to be creative she had moved directly to the throat and was in effect expressing nothing creative. It was the voice of communication in her sacral that led her to seek help. She needed an empathic listening ear as well as healing to resolve her difficulties.

A person sought healing for bad headaches and stomach pain that seemed to originate at the workplace. He had seen his doctor and was given a pain-relieving prescription and a checkup with a specialist. Nothing seemed to be wrong with him. The client wondered if there could have been environmental problems caused by lighting, using

The color of the chakras is of immense importance for a healer in assessing a person's emotional state.

computers, air quality, and so on, but as he thought through these factors he felt that none of them was the cause of the headaches.

Looking at the solar plexus chakra revealed a screen that was ragged at the edges with black lines crisscrossing a pale insipid yellow background. During the healing session, the client said that he had a number of worries about his work and had come to the conclusion that he actually feared going to work. His solar plexus chakra, impacting on the nearby organs of the body, was doing its best to get him to ask himself some searching questions about

his work and direction in which his life was taking. A series of healing sessions helped him to sort his worries, and each time he was able to check out his progress through the energetic scanning.

Findings like these are an important element in your database to which you can constantly refer. By comparing the life issues that each chakra processes and linking them with their color vibrations (see table The Chakras and their Related Life Issues on page 23), a remarkable picture emerges of the workings of the chakras in the mental and emotional lives of your clients.

Auras are seen as areas of colored light around a person. These colors change as mood or pattern of thinking changes.

The Role of Healing in Serious and Terminal Illness

The role of spiritual healing in life-threatening and terminal illness is to provide an atmosphere of peace and harmony where the patient can rest and feel safe. This enables patients to use the healing energies in the way most appropriate for them, as distinct from what may be desired by loved ones or caregivers.

In the case of terminal illness, healing offers the patient the opportunity to become used to moving out of the physical body and to experience the consciousness of peace without any of the symptoms of the condition or possible side effects of medication.

During spiritual healing it is common for the patient to fall into a "healing sleep." This is the condition where the patient quite naturally and easily leaves the physical body to enhance the healing. When the terminally ill person returns from the healing sleep and says that he/she did not want to come back, it is a sign that he/she is having a good experience in learning how to move into the next phase of life. Many come to understand that there is no death, merely the dropping of the physical body that is no longer serving him.

Doctors and nursing staff in hospices and hospital wards are quite used to patients talking to themselves or seeming to be in their own dream world. Here they are talking to or communicating with relatives and friends in spirit form who have come to spend time with them to help them with the process of passing over.

Healers always find it a privilege to work with the terminally ill. They witness the beauty and courage of another human being who is facing the unknown and becoming aware of the energetic changes going on as the individual soul withdraws from the level of the physical.

Working as a spiritual healer in hospitals and hospices is generally welcomed by staff, but it should be done only with their express permission ...

Spiritual healing for the terminally ill can enable a peaceful passing over without pain or the need for medication.

Healing energy is never wasted. In these situations, the patient is using the energy in ways that may not always be apparent to an onlooker. Many people who have a terminal illness, or who have endured much suffering, become weakened during the final stages of life and utilize the energy to pass over.

Working as a spiritual healer in hospitals and hospices is generally welcomed by staff, but it should be done only with their express permission and, of course, at the request of the patient.

The Energetic Situation

It would be unusual for a healer to be able to give a full healing session in a hospital. Your work would probably be confined to holding the patient's hand or holding your hands near some point on the patient's body. Even in these circumstances healers may get a sense of the patient's energy field. In serious and terminal illness, the whole subtle-energy system is found to be far less anchored to the physical and may be sensed as hovering a little above the body. The field has a tendency to contract, with less power in the lower three chakras. The base chakra in

particular would be very low in energy. However, the field around the crown chakra often seems to have increased—an indication that soul activity is enhanced.

The Effects of the Healing Atmosphere

The situation around a terminally ill person often highlights the conflicts that exist in the relationships between relatives and friends. Suddenly everyone is challenged to face the truth about their ability to love unconditionally.

As well as providing a special atmosphere for the patient, spiritual healers create a space where relatives and friends of the patient can receive healing for the distress they are experiencing. The healing atmosphere also encourages people to settle their differences, air problems, and look at relationships from a fresh perspective. This is where healing energies demonstrate that they are in fact another form of love, that love is an energy that can be given or witheld.

When, for whatever reason, it is not possible to be physically present with a patient, distant healing may be offered (see pages 114–119).

Death, Loss, and Bereavement

We are soul, or spirit, and soul cannot die. What dies is the body that has served its soul purpose. Once the body is no longer able to absorb the life force, every cell begins the process of breaking the body down into its chemical components so that they can be returned to the earth.

We pass back to the realm of spirit from where we came. Having discarded the body, a person does not feel any of the pain or trauma that may have been experienced prior to death.

We are helped to make the transition by loved ones or other beings in spirit. Many people need special help to understand what has happened to them, especially those who have died a very sudden or violent death. This help is always provided, but it is so common for people to be confused about their death that those on earth who have the ability may do what is known as rescue work.

A passing may be difficult or impossible to understand for those left behind. The role of the healer very often extends from dealing with the terminal illness to helping clients and their relatives and friends cope with death and its aftermath of bereavement. Anyone involved in bereavement, including the healer, is inevitably affected by his or her own pattern of loss.

Loss

Life can seem like a series of deaths or losses, because change, which is the essence of life, is a constant process of renewal. As we change and life changes around us, we lose our past selves, our experiences, our surroundings, our health, ways of being, friends, and so on. No one is exempt from loss, but every person will react in a different way in this situation.

Energetically, loss affects many chakras. Change may threaten a person's sense of security. This registers in the base chakra. Another person finds that all the joy has gone out of life and creativity is shelved. The sacral chakra registers this response. People who have undergone severe trauma may be affected in the throat or brow, unable to speak or unable to see. If imbalance persists, when a person cannot process the loss, for example, the energetic situation quickly moves to affect the mental or emotional levels or the impact on the body creates a physical condition.

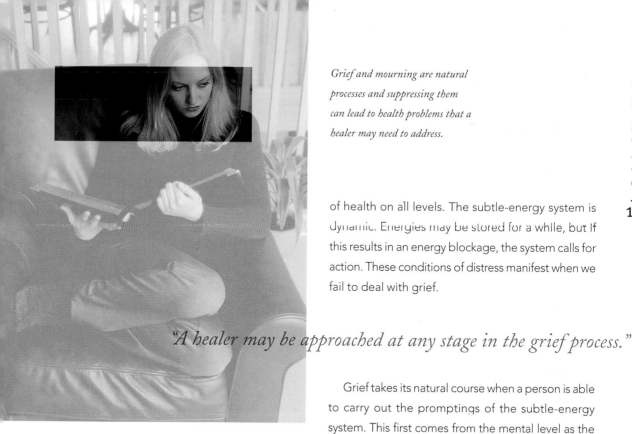

Grief and mourning are natural processes and suppressing them can lead to health problems that a healer may need to address.

of health on all levels. The subtle-energy system is dynamic. Energies may be stored for a while, but If this results in an energy blockage, the system calls for action. These conditions of distress manifest when we fail to deal with grief.

"A healer may be approached at any stage in the grief process."

Most loss reactions are registered in the heart chakra because they are about the loss of a loved one, a love relationship, a loved thing, a place, or a memory. These are often difficult to process because of the grief involved. A person's reaction may affect the thymus gland and the immune system, resulting in conditions ranging from a common cold to a serious illness such as cancer.

Healing to the subtle-energy system is required, as well as skilled and empathic counseling.

Grief and Mourning

Grief is the energy of loss, and mourning is the task that loss sets us. Mourning is a natural part of human experience, but its essential place in life may be overlooked or forgotten. The findings of spiritual healing illustrate that unprocessed grief is a destroyer

Grief takes its natural course when a person is able to carry out the promptings of the subtle-energy system. This first comes from the mental level as the need to accept that the loss has happened. Often the shock of loss is too great and we go into denial or disbelief. Next is the challenge of the emotional level to live with the pain of the grief. The body then demands that we live with the fact that who or what is lost is no longer there. This again is a huge challenge. We may not want to live with this demand. If people manage to deal with these three aspects of grief, healing can then help them to try to begin a new life.

A healer may be approached at any stage in the grief process. By carefully listening to the client's story it is possible to locate where the person is in terms of mourning and to see if this is corroborated by the energy scans and healings. We have described what occurs energetically, but there is no logical sequence of events in grief and bereavement. Your role is to be there for the client, to help her to find her way through, to provide a safe place to "contain" her as the necessary disintegration and readjustment to life takes place.

Distant Healing

If you have managed to carry out all the exercises so far and you have had plenty of practice with a partner, you may feel that you are ready to work with other people. But you have not yet joined an organization, a healing center, or group, and no one knows you are out there. However, you can practice distant healing. This is a way of working when the client is at a distance from the healer. For the healer who has no clients it is a way of attuning and keeping the channel open. It is so effective that some healers either specialize in distant healing or have it as part of their practice.

Healing energies originate and travel outside the space/time framework of the physical so they are not limited by distance or time. Therefore the healer is able to transmit spiritual energies, even when physical distance prevents the usual "hands-on" approach. Typical situations occur when the client cannot travel—because of disability, distance,

about this issue by the end of the chapter. It is a good idea to involve the person concerned; this can be done by asking him to let you know at regular intervals how he is progressing. A further empowering step is to ask him to tune in to your distant-healing session. Ask him to sit or lie in a comfortable position and relax at the same time as you are attuning to him. The person should visualize a golden bubble of protective light around him and stay like this for 10–15 minutes. Tell him that you would welcome any comments about the session.

You do not need to know about the person's condition, but it may help him if he describes it to you. You are going to send healing to the person, not the condition. How the person uses the energy will be a decision made at a soul level. You are concerned with offering the help and not with the outcome. This is the attitude you need to have in all your healing efforts and it especially applies in distant work.

"Healing energies originate and travel outside the space/time framework of the physical so they are not limited by distance or time."

confinement, illness, pregnancy, or hospitalization. Or it may be that the healer is not able to travel. But in all cases the healer can offer distant healing.

Most people ask for distant healing themselves, but you may be asked to send your help to a third party. Some healers decide that they will work only with someone who has asked for help and do not feel it is ethical if that person does not know. You must make up your own mind, but see what you think

The reason is that the transmission of energy is initiated by your intention. Spiritual healing has the holistic vision of the whole person, not a manifestation of an energetic state or a diagnosis based on symptoms. By directing healing to the person you are not limiting the activities of the energies in any way.

The following exercise is a simple way to conduct a session of your own. Keep a note of the work just as you would with a healing practice.

Exercise 28:
A Distant-Healing Session

Compile a short list of people who have asked for healing. Bring that with you to the exercise. Choose a time when you will not be disturbed. Disconnect or switch off telephones. Carry out the full attunement process as on page 61. Prepare a room or a corner of a room as a distant-healing sanctuary. This might include a small table with a candle.

1 Sit in a comfortable chair in which you can keep a straight back with your feet flat on the floor. Your hands should be palms-up on your thighs. If necessary, take a few full breaths to center yourself.

2 Light the candle and dedicate the light to the work. See this as the Light of healing. Take the light into your heart center and allow it to spread out into your chest. Give thanks for the opportunity to work in this way. Ask for protection for yourself and for the people on the list. This part of the exercise is attuning you to that person, creating the Healing Triangle.

3 Have your list ready so that you can read it aloud or mentally. The name of the person is the vibratory link with you and the healing.

Ask for healing for each named person in turn: "I ask for healing for… [name], for… [name]" etc. As you say the name, visualize the person put into the Light of healing.

4 When you have come to the end of the list, give your thanks and close your session in your own way. The light of the candle could be sent out to where it is needed.

Do not forget to practice the closing-down exercises described on pages 85–87, either after your session or before retiring.

Distant Healing with a Group

The energy generated by a group can be very powerful. Distant healing is an excellent addition to the work of a healing, prayer, or meditation group. Remember not to name the problem or illness—because that makes the work conditional. By the time the group has heard a list of problems and illnesses, the energies will have been considerably lowered!

Exercise 29: A Group Distant-Healing Session

Prepare the room as a sacred space. Ask each group member to bring a list of people for distant-healing (the group may need to agree on a certain number to fit the available time). Have a small table with a candle in the center of the room. Arrange the chairs around the table. Choose someone to lead the session and give instructions. Leadership should vary at each meeting so that all members have a turn. The exercise begins with a group attunement.

The group could begin their attunement standing, with Exercise 10, "The Rainbow Breath"(page 43). Then everyone sits comfortably in a circle with feet flat on the floor and hands palms-up resting on the thighs. For the purpose of the exercise, the following are the instructions for the group.

1 We are going to breathe in the energies of love and peace (as in Exercise 16, "Breathing Love and Peace", page 63). This may be visualized as a vivid pink light. With the in-breath, let the energy of love fill the heart center. With the out-breath let go of anxieties, worries, and any unloving thoughts or situations. Taking as many breaths as you need, allow the energy of love to fill the rest of your body and then to fill the healing sanctuary. Take a few moments to feel the atmosphere of love around the group.

2 Now we breathe in the energy of peace. This may be visualized as a pure white light. With the in-breath, let the energy of peace fill the heart center. With the out-breath let go of any disturbing feelings or disruptive thoughts. Allow the energy of peace to fill the rest of your body and then to fill the healing sanctuary. Take a few moments to feel the atmosphere of peace around the group.

3 [The leader lights the candle and dedicates it to the work of the group.] Focus on the light of the candle and draw the light into your heart center. Realizing this as the center of unconditional love, pass the love to the person on your left. Feel the energy of love moving around the group, uniting everyone.

4 [The leader says any prayers of gratitude, dedication, and protection. Other members of the group who need to pray aloud should follow. This completes the group's attunement to the Source and each other.]

5 I am going to read out my list. Please visualize each person named being placed in the Light in the center of our circle. When I have finished my list, the signal for the person on my left to start will be when I say, "Thank you." I ask for healing for… [name], etc.

6 [Each group member reads out his or her list without mentioning any conditions.]

7 See all those we have mentioned being cared for in the light of love, peace, and healing. I now close the healing circle with thanks on behalf of all of us. Before we send out the Light, would anyone like to say anything else? [Leader allows space.] Would anyone like to send out the Light? [A group member sends out the Light by saying to whom or where it is going while extinguishing the candle flame.] The leader should then encourage any comments or discussion about the group's experiences. The meeting can close once the group has carried out the closing down procedures on pages 85–87.

Distant Healing: Taking It Further

Astral-Healing

It is quite usual for healers to move out of the physical body when sending distant healing to another person. Many people testify to seeing the healer visit them to give them healing. Conversely, it is quite normal for the person in question to be transported in the astral body to the healer.

Astral traveling takes place when a person moves out of the physical body to travel, unencumbered by it, in the astral body, which is the subtle-energy form used for this purpose. Astral traveling is simply traveling anywhere outside the physical level. The term is derived from the Latin and Greek for star. The most common form of astral traveling is that which we all do in the sleep state, so to the ancients it was as if each night we traveled among the stars.

Astral work is quite safe as long as your attunement is in place. When in the learning stage, work with a partner who can monitor your progress.

Other Applications of Distant Healing

The natural world, the environment, and situations nearby or on the other side of the planet are all in need of our help. This is where you can be of service again, keeping your channel open and keeping yourself attuned to the Source, to Oneness.

Take time to think about all the places and situations where healing is needed. It may be something you have seen in the newspaper or on television or a disaster or problem you have heard about. You can do something to restore balance and harmony. Read back through Exercise 28, "A Distant-Healing Session" (page 115), and create your new healing list. It can include the animal and plant world too. Once you have experienced how easy it is to do this you can send healing thoughts right away, wherever you are.

You are becoming a healing presence. You are recreating the healing channel.

Exercise 30:
An Astral-Healing Session

Prepare yourself as in Exercise 28, "A Distant-Healing Session"(page 115). Once you are confident that you can work this way and that you enjoy doing it, compile a short list of people who have asked for healing and bring it with you to the session. For the purpose of the exercise, work with one person only. Choose a time when you will not be disturbed. Disconnect or switch off telephones or other things that might disturb you. Prepare a room or a corner of a room as a distant-healing sanctuary. This area might contain a small table with a candle. Ask your partner to monitor what happens.

1 Sit in a comfortable chair in which you can keep a straight back with your feet flat on the floor. Your hands should be palms-up on your thighs. If necessary, take a few full breaths to center yourself.

2 Light the candle and dedicate the light to the distant-healing work. See this light as the Light of healing. Take the light into your heart center and allow it to spread out into your chest. Give thanks for the opportunity to work in this way. Ask for protection for yourself and the person on your list. You are attuning to that person and creating the Healing Triangle.

3 The name of the person is the vibratory link with you and the healing. Ask for healing for the named person: "I ask for healing for… [name]." Now wait patiently. If you are suited to astral work, you will feel the healing signal (such as tingling) in your hands and sense that the person has been brought to you to work on. The person will probably be lying down as if on the healing couch. What do your hands want to do? Do not rely on a routine but simply go to work as you feel directed by soul.

4 You will sense when the healing is complete and that the "client" is no longer present for you. Give your thanks and close the session in your own way. The light of the candle could be sent out to where it is needed.

Discuss your experience with your partner. It would be very helpful for you to swap roles another time so that you can monitor the process too. Practice together the closing-down exercises on pages 85–87.

Creating the
Channel

alfway through this book you asked yourself: "Am I a healer?" and found a simple way to assess this. But your answer was just the beginning, not a definition of who you are for all time. Perhaps the rest of the book has shown you that healing is a process, a flow of energies, and a continuing opening of the heart. You can take healing as far as you want or you can relax and see where healing wants to take you.

This chapter is all about you and the vision you have of yourself. The exercises in the book so far will have shown you that spiritual healing is a complementary therapy in its own right, but it also offers anyone a special way of being as a person and as a carer. This is through its links to the sacred.

The holistic vision of spiritual healing is a celebration of Oneness and the oneness of all energy and energy patterns. Healing energy is continually available. We can be open to it or closed to it, tuned in to it or out of tune with it. Our way of being is the way we daily recreate ourselves and recreate the healing channel; therefore our way of being is the channel.

This is how and why the healing channel is enhanced through our own personal transformation as well as through our experience and our developing awareness.

So we will look at simple ways of making a sacred connection on a regular basis, ways of assessing psychic ability and intuitive awareness, ways of understanding the forces at work in your own practice, and ways of looking after yourself and your developing sensitivity.

Self-Development: Creating a Healing Lifestyle

An easy and effective way to create a healing lifestyle is to set up links with the sacred throughout the day, simple reminders about your relationship with the Source. Decide how you want your day to begin, what you want to put into it, and how you want it to end.

Sleep and Dreams

In the sleep state everyone leaves the body to travel in the subtle realms. Sleep is vital for resting and refreshing the physical body, but another important aspect of sleep is astral travel. Here we can meet souls from other realms as well as people here on earth who are also traveling out of their bodies. This facilitates important meetings with loved ones and friends; we can be reunited with those who have passed over and receive teachings that are not available to us in our daily lives. The brain tries to make sense of all these happenings and interprets them in the form of dreams.

When we wake up we have returned to body consciousness. We may have awakened naturally in our own time or have been awakened. In the latter case we need to realize that we may not be fully back in our bodies. We experience this as a range of reactions from a headache to feeling out of sorts or very grumpy. If this happens to you, take appropriate action before carrying on with normal waking life. Lie down again and relax. Take a few slow breaths. Now imagine yourself slowly re-entering your body through the top of your skull. Allow yourself to flow down to your feet. Wiggle your toes and fingers to check that you are "in place." A second way is to imagine that you are lowering your subtle (astral) body down to the physical body. Check your "landing." A final check is to imagine that your chakras are all aligned, as in a docking procedure! Try both ways to see which is most comfortable for you.

But you may be far more preoccupied by your dreams. Have a notebook by the bedside so that you can make a quick note of any dreams before they fade. The vivid ones are important and are probably messages from a soul level. Dreams are a wonderful way of developing the self, of studying our life journey, and of rediscovering our own wisdom. You might feel, therefore, that you would like to keep a separate dream journal. Perhaps you could join a group where dreams are explored. Take time to work with the dream material as in the next exercise.

Exercise 31:
Working with Dreams

1 Relax your body and breathe normally. Tell yourself that you are going to recall as much of the dream as possible. Know that, at some level, you know exactly what the dream is saying. You simply have to make yourself open to its meaning.

2 Recall the sequence of events or start from what you initially remember and build on that. Note the atmosphere of the story and how you felt in it, how you interacted with any other characters, and how they made you feel.

3 Having assembled what you can, you want to know what the dream means and what message it may hold. This is where literal ways of thinking may interfere. Dreams have their own logic, their own ways of speaking to us, and their own language. Let go and allow the dream to take you into its world. Be like the empathic listener that you have to be when working with a client.

4 Look at each character and situation in turn and let them talk to you. Sense again the atmosphere of the dream and let it talk to you. Be aware of how you felt in the dream and how you feel now.

5 A further approach is to ask yourself: if each person, animal, or thing in the dream is an aspect of you, what does that tell you?

Perhaps a dream has been upsetting or confusing. Try to hold this feeling as long as you can until you have unraveled the message. The feeling will disperse on its own. If it does not, you probably need to do some more work with your dream. But if you do not have the chance at this moment, lie or sit comfortably with your hands over your solar plexus chakra. Breathe light into the chakra until you feel calm returning. As you turn your attention to getting up, try the next exercise.

Exercise 32:
Acknowledging Relationship

1 You are breathing, taking in air and the life force. You are related to air, the wind, and the creatures of the air. Take a moment to acknowledge these things.

2 As your feet touch the floor you are reminded of your contact with the ground. You are aware of your body. It has been working for you all night. Your body has come from the earth. You are related to the landscape, the earth, and the earth family. Take a moment to acknowledge these things.

3 Notice how warm or how cold you are. Notice how light or dark it is around you and outside. Look for sources of light and sources of heat. You are related to the sun and to fire. Take a moment to acknowledge these things.

4 You turn on water to wash, brush your teeth, drink, or flush the toilet. Most of your body is made of water. You are related to water, to rain, to rivers and oceans, to the water creatures. Take a moment to acknowledge these things.

You are consciously acknowledging Oneness. Try your own version of acknowledgment. You might find that thanking comes into the picture.

A Broader View of Nutrition

We have to eat to live, which is a good reason for making mealtimes as enjoyable as possible. But from time to time healers need to review their overall nutrition as part of taking care of themselves.

What are we taking into the system in terms of food? Where does it come from and how was it produced? Questions like these require us to look at the energetic qualities of food. Many ancient cultures, such as the Indian culture, stressed the need to be aware of the consequences of introducing certain energies into our own system, especially if a person engages in a spiritual practice such as healing. For example, a food that has a light quality (such as a fresh leaf vegetable) will blend well with your body, but food with a heavy quality (such as overcooked or stale food) will burden it and take energy rather than give it.

Furthermore, as healers, we need to take a broader view of our nutrition, and to examine all its forms.

Exercise 33:
Acknowledging Nutrition

All levels of our being need feeding. This exercise uses the theme of the elements to link us to these levels. As you work through the points make notes for consideration later. Another approach would be to work with a partner and to discuss your findings together.

1 Fire is related to the spirit and the light in our life. What kind of light is there in your life? What makes you feel warm inside? What opens your heart like a flower opening to the sun? What is your daily experience of the sacred—your spiritual nourishment?

2 Air is related to the mind and the air we breathe. What sort of air do you breathe? What do you feed your mind with? What generates negative thinking in yourself? How do you react to negative thought forms? What is your mental nourishment?

3 Water is related to the emotions and the water of our bodies. What kind of water and other liquids do you drink? What makes you emotional? What do you feed your emotions with? What generates negative emotions in you. What is your emotional nourishment?

4 Earth is related to our bodies, nature, and the planet. Include the questions above about your food. What kind of environment do you live in and how do you relate to it? Have you found ways to recycle waste? Do you exercise? What is your total physical nutrition?

The ideas in this exercise are a beginning. Let them lead to your own broader consideration and discussions with others. For example, you could look at your relationship with the various elements.

Prayer: Making Space for the Sacred

Over two-thirds of our communication with others is nonverbal, and this is exactly how it is with prayer. Words are only a small part of the act of prayer.

The urge of the soul arises in the mind as the healing intention. Your intention immediately changes your energy field, opening it to the Light. In healing terms, this is the first stage of prayer.

As you set about attuning yourself to be a channel for healing, your body was engaging in prayer. Then, as you set about energizing the place where you were going to work, to align it with your intention, your body was again in a state of prayer. The healing room and your body thus became prayers. Prayer is a way of linking with and making space for the sacred. As part of your healing lifestyle, engage your creativity in making prayer—the hundred and one simple reminders about your relationship with the Source—as diverse as you can. Prayer is an experience. It is felt and it creates a special level of awareness that is the state of prayerfulness.

Most of us begin to pray with words—an inner acknowledgment that we can commune with the Source. A true prayer can be simply telling it how it is, like sharing with a close friend. Prayer links us with all humanity, for we all need to commune with our sense of the sacred. Prayer acknowledges that we all have deep needs.

Some of the most memorable prayers, such as the Prayer of St. Francis, express a profound wish to embody a certain way of being. In the words of the prayer we are telling ourselves: This is how I want to be. A prayer is a recognition of who we really are, for we are this vision of ourselves.

Here is an exercise where prayer can be sensed. Once the state of prayerfulness is entered, it may or may not give birth to words.

Lord, make me an instrument of your peace:
where there is hatred, let me sow love;
where there is injury, pardon;
where there is doubt, faith;
where there is despair, hope;
where there is darkness, light;
where there is sadness, joy.
Grant that I may not so much
seek to be consoled as to console;
to be understood, as to understand;
to be loved, as to love.
from the Prayer of St. Francis of Assisi
(1181–1226)

Exercise 34:
Prayer as Making Space

1 Sit comfortably in a peaceful place, if possible in a natural environment. Relax the body and take a number of full breaths to clear yourself, letting go on the out-breath. As you breathe in sacred breath, allow yourself to sink into Oneness. You are one with all that is around you. Acknowledge this.

2 Let your focus move to your base chakra. Your body has brought you to this place. Allow yourself to be aware of every sensation about your body and about your surroundings. Breathe your appreciation of your body into this center. Its prayer is: May this body be loved! Feel these words in your heart chakra.

3 Let your focus move to your sacral chakra. Breathe your appreciation of your surroundings into this center. Here is your center of joy. Its prayer is: May joy be released! Feel these words in your heart chakra.

4 Let your focus move to your solar plexus center. You are aware of your oneness with your surroundings. This is who you are. This oneness is your true source of power. Breathe this affirmation into your solar plexus. Its prayer is: I am! Feel these words in your heart chakra.

5 Return to your awareness of sacred breath. Each breath is a prayer that every being "hears." You are at the center of the space that your prayer has created.

Meditation: Entering the Silence

"Silence is the garden of meditation."
Ali (Ibn Abu Talib), **seventh century** CE

Creative activities can produce the right moment for meditation.

The previous exercise takes you to the space where you can enter into the Silence. This term for being at one with the sacred is common throughout the world. The Native American Cherokee people, for example, talk of being in the Great Silence. If prayer is a special state of awareness in which we give our energy to the divine, then meditation is a state of deep stillness where we are open and receptive. One state easily merges with the other.

Although the purpose of meditation is to be Oneness, attaining the stillness benefits all levels. Mental processes are brought to a halt, so mindsets and conditioning no longer influence us. Emotional processes are slowed down, and, as emotional reaction is quelled, we become aware of the language of soul—feelings. The body becomes relaxed and at peace. Physical and subtle energetic processes are calmed and balanced.

This calming of the levels has the healing effect of releasing stored, trapped, or blocked energies. It is quite natural for parts of the body to move involuntarily. Mental and emotional energies may be released as crying, laughter, and visual effects in the brain. It is most important to relax and let these things happen. They may or may not reveal to us their origin.

For the spiritual healer, the healing state is almost the same as the meditative state where the pattern of brain waves and other body energies have slowed down. This allows for soul connection and travel out of the body.

The purpose of meditation is to be at one with the sacred. Because we are already at one, the different ways are designed to trigger this awakening. For some this may happen without warning—the mind has moved out of consciousness, leaving space for soul. So you could be walking in nature, focusing on a task, doing something creative, making love, enjoying a meal, and so on. But when you link prayerful intention to any action, the meditative dimension is enhanced.

There are a thousand and one ways to pray and to meditate, and they do not all involve sitting still in a certain posture. Try various methods to see which you enjoy most. But give your chosen way a chance rather than hopping from one to another. Here is a simple way to enter the Garden of Silence.

Exercise 35:
Meditation: Entering the Silence

1 Sit somewhere peaceful and comfortable, inside or outside. Make sure that either the base of your spine or the soles of your feet are touching the ground. Keep your back straight with your hands resting lightly on your thighs. Take six full breaths into the heart center, relaxing the body and letting go of any problems or anxieties with the out-breath. Your purpose is to enter the Garden of Silence, the Presence of Oneness.

2 Listen to the sound of your breath as you breathe in and then out. Be aware that any other sounds you hear are accompanying you, they are part of sacred Oneness. Gently let your eyes close and allow your focus to remain in the heart center or the brow. Watch your inner screen in a totally relaxed way. Any thoughts, feelings, or sensations are simply accompanying you. Allow them to pass on their way as you gently hold your focus.

3 Rest in the Garden of Silence. You are home. You are safe.

4 When it is time to leave, close your meditation, making sure that you are well grounded (back in your body). Become aware of your feet and hands, your connection with the earth, and check your visual focus.

5 If you are beginning meditation, try this exercise for about 10 minutes. Build it up to 30 minutes, twice a day. Your first session should be as early in your day as possible. It will form a foundation for your healing lifestyle.

As we mentioned above, prayer and meditation are complementary energy flows between ourselves and the Source. You may find that the end of a meditation session flows back into the prayer state. The prayer state is a heart-centered state so this is a natural place for expressions of gratitude and for blessing. Giving thanks keeps the cycle of giving and receiving moving.

A blessing clears and balances anything, such as a meal, bringing it into harmony with your own energies. This is the origin of saying grace at mealtimes. A blessing from you to another clears the way for that person, bringing peace and harmony. A blessing is first of all a mental intention, an inner impulse. It can be given as such or you may need to verbalize it and even use your body to reinforce the blessing intention.

More Self-Awareness: Assessing your Day

After work you can take time to write up your journal, go through it, and maybe take a look at your dream journal too. As you look at your day as a whole, perhaps patterns have emerged.

Looking at Reality

It is tempting to think that we are victims of circumstances, but the law of energy is that we all create our own reality. The soul exerts an influence moment by moment and the mind interprets this as thought and a plan of action. The body carries out the action and our feelings tell us whether we like it or otherwise. Here are some key points to consider.

Exercise 36:
Assessing your View of Reality

1 In a comfortable position, relax and consider the points in this exercise as if you can see yourself from a distance, without judgment and without bending the truth.

2 What reality did you create today? Spend a few moments checking out your day as if watching a video of it. Is there a link between your reactions to happenings and your reality?

3 How has your spiritual healing work or learning fit into the picture?

4 Your reality is a reflection of how you perceive yourself and the reality that your clients describe is a picture of how they perceive themselves. Even if you have not worked with anyone today, recall any phrases that you have heard others uttering. How far do you think their way of speaking is a true reflection of their inner being?

5 When you look at what you have thought about others, does this have anything to say about you?

Our daytime activities affect us during sleep, and solutions to problems will emerge as we connect with soul knowledge.

This exercise offers you a picture of the energies that you have sent out into the world today and the way you use energy in terms of love and its opposite, fear. If you can get a partner to do a separate self-assessment, meet up for a mutual sharing of the implications for both of you.

The exercise has nothing to do with morality. There is no right or wrong way to be. If your prayers have been describing the person that you know you really are, does the way you use energy serve your highest purpose?

Preparing for Sleep

Any healing or spiritual work that you have done today will have opened your chakras. Before retiring to sleep, bring your subtle-energy system back to everyday functioning. To do this carry out Exercise 15, "Clearing the Energy Field" (page 61), Exercise 21, "Regulating the Chakras" (page 86), and Exercise 22, "The Sphere of Protection" (page 87).

Whatever is in your mind will continue affecting you in the sleep state. Television, conversations, reading matter, thought patterns, and emotional reactions all create related energetic forms. You have a choice about what type of nourishment you will give to your sleep. Of course this can be used beneficially to solve problems. The term "sleep on it" describes the fact that, during the sleep state, the mind can receive the benefit of soul knowledge to which it was closed during the day. When you are wrestling with a problem, relax and hand it over to this higher authority, confident that it will be solved while you sleep. The next day, as long as you stay away from the worried state, you will receive the solution to this problem.

As far as dreams are concerned, sleep is the start of a new day. Material will be sorted and processed and any messages needed for the next day will be created, usually in symbolical or allegorical form (a language of pictures and feelings). These will be conveyed to the mind and then the brain for interpretation. In emergencies we may be awoken during sleep. A nightmare needs careful attention since its message may range from "Please do not eat doughnuts at bedtime" to a clear warning about a life situation. Keep your dream journal handy along with a pencil.

A final thought of thanks for your day, no matter what it has brought you, keeps a flow of positivity throughout the night. These are the ideal conditions for soul knowledge and intuitive awareness to flourish.

Your Third Eye: Intuitive and Psychic Awareness

Throughout the book you have been engaging the sensing aspects of your brow chakra—your intuitive and psychic awareness. These two natural human faculties have for centuries been jointly known as the Third Eye. The brow chakra allows us to sense or "see" subtle energies and energetic effects both within and outside ourselves. Energies outside us, such as another person's aura, have come to be known as psychic phenomena. Inside effects, such as information from a soul level, are termed intuitive. All of us are aware in these ways, though we may not be conscious of it. As you have discovered, spiritual healers work consciously with the different functions of both these faculties.

Psychic Awareness

The most commonly known brow chakra activity is the ability to process subtle energetic effects and to convey this information to the mind and brain for interpretation. When the brain interprets the effect visually it is called clairvoyance. Everyone has his or her own way of sensing and interpreting, so some may describe their awarenesses as sound or sensation or an inner knowing. In the early exercises you were building confidence in your own psychic awareness (as in Exercise 2, "Sensing the Aura with a Partner" (page 19), and Exercise 3, "Locating the Major Chakras" (page 26). To enhance your attunement with another, as you sit opposite that person, let your sight relax and see if you can detect the etheric body. This

may seem like a layer of light extending 1–2 inches (2–5 cm) beyond the physical. Once you are successful with this, if only for a moment, let your relaxed vision move beyond the etheric to the whole of the other person's field. Keep a note of what you see or sense now.

Intuitive Awareness

The other complementary function of the brow chakra provides a center for the input of soul knowledge and wisdom. This too is a form of seeing or sensing. Here, we engage with energies on the mental, emotional, etheric, and physical levels but

*It is important for a healer
to gain attunement with the client
so that the healing is directed by
soul rather than ego.*

they are first interpreted by soul, or in their spiritual context. Soul's perception may then be passed on as feeling rather than mental material with which we are already familiar.

Mind can only compare information with what is already in its data bank. This is why we so often disregard our intuition because it does not check out with mind. Later we may realize that our first impulse was the correct one.

Spiritual healers need to make contact with their own soul and with the soul of the client. This is attunement and it ensures that the healing session will be directed by soul and not by the egos of the healer and/or the client. So a healer learns to trust soul guidance and encourages and empowers the client to do the same. The healer knows that clients heal themselves if they are given the necessary energetic environment where they can discover faith in their own being. On some level the healing encounter is a meeting of souls and it is the client's reconnection with the sacred that initiates healing, whether or not the person is conscious of this.

In Exercise 17, "Attunement to Another Person" (page 64), and Exercise 19, "Healing with the Client on a Couch" (page 72), you were linking with your brow chakra and allowing soul information to guide you.

This was made possible by your attunement. When you find yourself receiving information during the scans or during the third part of the healing procedure, it may be through your psychic awareness. But you may also receive information passed to you by soul. Thus intuition, when used by the healer, enhances communication with the various aspects of the client's subtle anatomy.

Experimenting to Develop the Subtle Senses

It is time to join with your partner again to experiment with your psychic and intuitive awareness until you are both confident that you know the difference and can consciously work with both faculties.

First, return to Exercise 2, "Sensing the Aura with a Partner" (page 19). This time stand together and find the extent of your partner's aura. Then allow your hands to move over its energy surface. Focus on your brow chakra and the impressions you receive rather than the sensation of the hand moving over the aura.

Now carry out your attunement and repeat the experiment. This time your soul is talking about what you are sensing. Was there any difference?

Understanding Patterns in your Work

As well as enhancing your healing abilities and daily life, developing your subtle awareness helps you to sense if there is a pattern of work evolving. Every healer attracts certain clients because he or she is the right therapist for that person at that particular time. You have something to offer which that person needs; the law of energy has brought you together. When you understand this you can work with the presenting condition without feeling inadequate or lacking in relevant experience. When you are assessing the session as objectively as possible you can make a decision about referring the client on. It would be natural for you to ask yourself sometimes: Why did this person choose me? The answer from a soul level might be: Why not you?

"I had many encounters with nature spirits, the spirits of animals and trees, which seemed to me perfectly normal."

People come for healing at major transitional points in their lives. Sometimes the pattern reflects the change in the seasons—winter depression or feelings of something dying as summer comes to an end, for example.

When assessing the overall pattern of a week's work, we find that every client is saying something to us. What has been their unspoken message? Again, have your clients been mirroring what is happening in the world. What is the message for you then?

Adding Other Skills

When I began healing, much of my work was at a distance. This gave me scope to reconnect with the subtle awareness I had as a small child. But it was not long before I noticed that most of the people who wanted to see me had emotional and/or mental problems and many of their physical conditions seemed to originate at these levels. I knew the work of psychotherapists and counselors and realized that I could be far more effective if I had some of the skills that they had.

Person-centered counseling, as developed by the late Carl Rogers in the United States, was the perfect complement to spiritual healing. This empathic counseling approach gives clients "unconditional positive regard" and states that they have their own answer to their presenting issue. One of the roles of

The world of nature can provide the opportunity to discover new ways of healing and of embracing one's natural self.

This gave me a profound love for the natural world, but a lot of pain whenever I witnessed it being abused or thoughtlessly destroyed.

In later life, working with a number of Native American medicine people encouraged me to look again at what they called natural spirituality—experiencing the sacred in nature. I rediscovered and reconnected with the huge affinity between healing and nature. This offers a whole new area of work—the opportunity of working with the land itself, and more, the opportunity of working with people in a natural setting. Here, people are able to celebrate being close to the elements and discover a new method of embracing their natural selves. These are healing ways.

You do not have to go to another country for the land to speak to you. You do not have to take on the ways of another culture to hear the voice of the earth family in your heart. If this is an area that calls to you, get started. Ask for help, listen to your heart/intuition for what to do next. Even in the depths of the city, Oneness is always present as earth, or creative nature.

the counselor, therefore, is to help the client to reach that place of awareness. I also found that the person-centered approach opens up the person's subtle-energy field so that healing can begin during the interview stage.

Healing will take you on an adventure of discovery and self-discovery, but be open to what healing is showing you. Do you need new skills that you can "bolt-on" to spiritual healing? Would you actually like to go down a totally new road?

Natural Spirituality

I grew up in the country and was lucky to be able to spend whole days just being with nature. I had many encounters with nature spirits, the spirits of animals and trees, which seemed to me perfectly normal.

Taking Care of Yourself

The difficulty many carers and therapists have is recognizing that they too need regular doses of tender loving care. You must always be alert to symptoms of stress and burnout. These can range from physical problems, such as poor digestion, lack of interest in exercise or sex, to irritability, touchiness, the need to cry for no apparent reason, to depression and feeling that meaning has gone out of life, to compassion fatigue.

Self-Protection

Emotional and mental energies impact on the solar plexus chakra. When people are feeling vulnerable in this way it is common to see them cross their arms over the solar plexus or hold a cushion there. We can protect ourselves energetically and avoid having our own energies absorbed by other people with a simple safety first measure.

The Power of Thought Forms

It is worth remembering that thoughts become things. Because energy follows thought, what you think you create. Furthermore, thoughts are energy patterns that attract related thought patterns to them. In this way, large blocks of similar thoughts exist on the subtle levels.

We are all affected by this phenomenon, and as a healer you are vulnerable because you are sensitive and very often open to other people's energies. If you think in a certain way you will attract that particular thought block to you. This is fine when you are feeling positive, but when you have feelings such as despondency, fear, or resentment, you draw similar thoughts to you. Before you are aware of it, you are feeling worse. The thought block has settled into your aura at a mental level and its energies are moving quickly into your consciousness, changing your emotional and physical balance. With practice and awareness you can stop this process at an early stage.

Exercise 37: The Solar Disk

1 Sit or lie comfortably. Relax and breathe normally. Let your breath focus on your solar plexus chakra. Without judgment or criticism, allow any impressions from this center to pass through your consciousness. Are there traces of fear or anxiety?

2 Now visualize a large golden disk covering your center. Is it quite plain or does it have any design on it? This is your personal solar disk and you can put it in place whenever you need it, wherever you are.

3 If you are in an emotional state yourself, your energies will quickly drain from you. Make the choice to put your solar disk in place as a first step to restoring balance.

Healers and other carers need to maintain inner balance consciously and find ways to recharge their batteries. This is all part of looking after yourself. There is a number of energizing and balancing exercises in the book (such as Exercise 11, "Breathing Color to Balance the Chakras," and Exercise 12, "Breathing in Vitality Energy"), but there is no better place to find both fresh energy and balance than in a natural or green place.

Exercise 38:
Breathing Green to Recharge and Rebalance

If possible find a peaceful place in green surroundings.

1 Sit comfortably on or near the ground and relax. Make sure that either the base of your spine or the soles of your feet are touching the ground. Breathe normally. Take three full breaths and become aware of your breathing. Let go and relax with the out-breath. Relax your mind. Just let thoughts come and go as they please without linking in with them.

2 Look around you. Identify the green—the grass, the trees, the bushes, the shrubs. Wait until a certain plant or patch of plants calls to you. With relaxed vision see the green of these plants as energy, as light. This special green light is what you need.

3 Breathe this light into your heart center. Know that it is bringing balance and energy to your system. When you feel that the heart center is full, allow the green light to fill your body.

4 Breathe normally, staying with the green. You are calm and centered. When you feel ready to leave, become aware of your feet and your body. Thank the plants and this place for their offerings.

5 If you are unable to get to a natural green place, make yourself ready as above. Focus on your heart chakra and ask to be shown the green light that you need. Proceed to breathe this light as directed in the exercise. Before you leave you could review how you have progressed with this book and where it has taken you on your way to this peaceful place, which you have blessed and which has blessed you.

If spiritual healing is going to be part of your life adventure, may it add extra color and joy.

Glossary

Astral: any **subtle level** of being outside of the **physical**. The astral body is the energy pattern that **soul** uses to travel on levels outside of the body, as when we are asleep, for example.

Astral-healing: healing where either or both healer and client are in their astral bodies, rather than their physical bodies. This allows the healer to easily "travel" to the client and vice versa.

Aura: the total energetic emanation of a person, which can be sensed as an energy field around the body. The traditional name for the human energy field, from the Greek, *avra*, meaning "breeze."

Center: see chakra.

Chakra: an **etheric** energy center, a point of energy concentration within the **subtle energy system**. Each chakra has a specific function (as outlined herein). From Sanskrit, *chakram*, a wheel (because ancient Indian seers saw that the whirling vortices of energy in the main chakras gave the impression of a turning cartwheel).

Channel: a conduit for the transmission of healing and other **subtle energies**. A person who is such a conduit.

Distant healing: healing given when the client is too far away to be accessible to **"hands-on" healing**.

Ego: the physical personality with its thoughts, emotions, and behavior. The ego tends to think and act as if it is the true person and finds it difficult to accept that it is actually the vehicle through which soul (who we really are) expresses itself.

Emotional: pertaining to the emotions and feelings. In healing, a level of energy frequency vibrating much faster than the physical or the etheric, but slower than the **mental**. Feelings are the language of soul and help us to sense what is "good" and "bad" for us.

Etheric: the subtle level of being that acts as a bridge between the physical and spiritual levels of energetic frequency (vibrations). The etheric body, the communication vehicle for the soul, is the place where the **chakras** are first detected.

Hands-on healing: healing that takes place when the healer uses hands either on or, more usually, near the body.

Holistic: in spiritual healing, the approach that sees humans as multidimensional beings, within a cosmic setting of animals, plants, and planet, all of which are part of the divine whole (**Oneness**).

Incarnation: birth on the earth plane so that soul can encounter and express itself through physical life.

Karma: the balancing law of cause and effect. Every action has an equal and opposite reaction. The theory that we are subject to this law while living a life on earth. We may, therefore, wish to "balance" the effects of our actions. This may mean returning to the earth plane in another lifetime (**see reincarnation**). From the Sanskrit root, *kar*, to do.

Level: a plane of being; a state of consciousness; a level of energy frequency (vibration). For example, the mental level is where we process thought.

Life force: the vital subtle energy essential to life. Sanskrit, *prana*; Chinese, *qi*. It is present in air and is taken into the bloodstream via the breath.

Light: with a capital letter, healing energy; the Source.

Mental: pertaining to mind and thought. In healing, it is a level of energy frequency which is much faster than the etheric and the physical.

Oneness: with a capital letter, the sacred unity of all that is. The Source. In Western religious terms, it is seen as God. In lower case, the fact of all things being part of a whole or the One.

Personality: the person we seem to be, the ego, which feels separate from the Source.

Physical: the level of energy vibration within the physical universe. The earth plane. We have a physical body so that we can experience life at this level.

Psychic: a subtle energetic happening outside a person. The sense of the brow chakra. A person who senses in this way.

Reincarnation: being born more than once on the earth plane. There is growing evidence for the actuality of this occurrence.

Sacred: pertaining to soul. The divine reality. What a person considers is holy or most precious to them.

Soul: in absolute terms, Oneness, God. In relative terms, the individual who we really are.

Glossary

Source: in this book, Oneness, God. The source of all that is; the source of all energy.

Spirit: the energy of the Source. A soul.

Spiritual: the experience of the sacred. A person's spiritual life is about what they do to experience the sacred.

Spiritual healing: soul-based **subtle energy medicine**. A healing modality using **subtle energies** that are acknowledged to have a divine or sacred origin. The ultimate purpose of spiritual healing is a spiritual one, being a way of helping a person to reconnect with their own spirituality and the sacred in life, and so promoting healing.

Subtle: of energy, traveling at a velocity beyond the speed of light. Humans (as well as animals and plants) are nevertheless equipped to sense these subtle energies.

Subtle energies: The energies used in healing, at all levels of our being. They are stepped down in frequency, by the chakras, for use at a physical level, where they are also easy to sense.

Subtle energy medicine: a healing modality that uses energies traveling at speeds

beyond the velocity of light (subtle energies). This modality includes such complementary therapies as spiritual healing, sound healing, color healing, reflexology, and the use of flower essences.

Subtle energy system: the total energetic structure of a person (including the etheric body and the chakras, the mental and emotional zones of the energy field) that enables soul to be embodied and to fully experience physical life.

Further Reading

Angelo, Jack. *Hands-On Healing*. Rochester, VT. Healing Arts Press, 1997.

Angelo, Jack. *Your Healing Power*. London: Piatkus Books, 2001.

Coates, Margrit. *Healing for Horses*. London: Rider, 2001.

Gerber, Richard. *Vibrational Medicine*. Santa Fe, NM: Bear & Company, 2001.

Kubler-Ross, Elisabeth & Kessler, David. *Life Lessons*. Touchstone Books, 2001.

Kubler-Ross, Elisabeth. *On Death and Dying*. New York: Macmillan, 1970.

Leadbeater, C.W. *The Chakras*. Wheaton, IL: Theosophical Publishing House, 1985.

Rinpoche, Sogyal. *The Tibetan Book of Living and Dying*. London: Rider, 1992.

Walsch, Neale Donald. *Friendship With God*. London: Hodder Mobius, 2000.

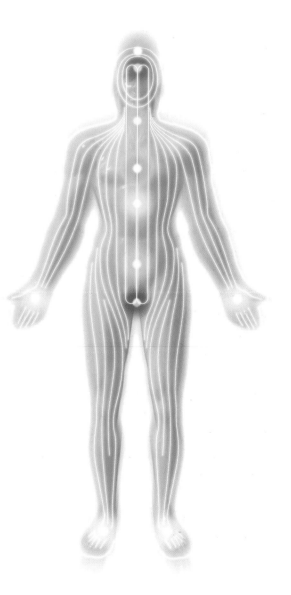

Useful Addresses

UK

British Association for Counselling and Psychotherapy (BACP)
1 Regent Place
Rugby
Warwicks CV21 2PJ
Tel: 8704 435252

British Association for the Person-Centered Approach (BAPCA)
BM BAPCA
London WC1N 3XX
Tel: 01989 770948

College of Healing
Runnings Park
Croft Bank
West Malvern
Worcs WR14 4DU
Tel: 01684 566450

College of Psychic Studies
16 Queensberry Place
London SW7 2EB
Tel: 020 7589 3292

Institute of Psychosynthesis
65a Watford Way, Hendon
London NW4 3AQ
Tel: 020 8202 4525

National Federation of Spiritual Healers (NFSH)
Old Manor Farm Studio
Church Street
Sunbury-on-Thames
Middlesex TW16 6RG
Tel: 01932 783164

Psychosynthesis and Education Trust
92–94 Tooley Street
London SE1 2TH
Tel: 020 7403 2100

White Eagle Lodge
New Lands
Brewells Lane
Liss
Hants GU33 7HY
Tel: 01730 893300

USA & Canada
American Society of Alternative Therapists
P.O. Box 703
Rockport, MA 01966

Association for Research and Enlightenment (ARE)
P.O. Box 595
Virginia Beach, VA 23451

Useful Addresses

Association of Spiritual Healers of Alberta
7535 Hunterview Drive NW
Calgary, Alberta
T2K 4P7 Canada

Barbara Brennan School of Healing
P.O. Box 2005
East Hampton, NY 11937

Center for Human Caring
University of Colorado School of Nursing
4200 East Ninth Avenue
Denver, CO 80262

Healing Heart Center
www.talamasca.org/avatar, a noncommercial
site dedicated to providing information
about alternative and spiritual healing.

Heart Awakening Project, Inc.
P.O. Box 4195
Cave Creek, AZ 85327
www.heartawakening.com

Institute of Neotic Sciences
474 Gate 5 Road, Suite 300
Sausalito, CA 94965

**International Society for the Study of
Subtle Energies and Energy Medicine
(ISSSEEM)**
11005 Ralston Road, Suite 100D
Arvada, CO 80004
www.issseem.org

Midwest Academy of Healing Arts
23534 Van Horn Road
Brownstone, MI 48134

One Star in Site
P.O. Box 390
Granger, IN 46530

Ontario Healers Network
3504/85 Thorncliffe Park Drive
Toronto, Ontario
M4H 1L4 Canada

Rose Lake Center for Natural Healing
7187 Drumheller Road
Bath, MI 48805

Touching Spirit Center
16 South Street
P.O. Box 337
Litchfield, CT 06759
www.touchingspirit.org

Wakepoint School of Energy Healing
660 Delmonico Drive, #272
Colorado Springs, CO 80919

Index

animals 100-101, 141
astral healing 118-119
attunement 60-61, 64-65, 68, 72, 79
aura 16-19, 133

babies 95
base chakra 23, 24, 29, 47, 49, 73, 79
bereavement 112-113
birth 94-95
body systems 33-47
breathing 40-43, 49, 50-51, 55, 63, 92-93, 137
brow chakra 23, 25, 28, 47, 49, 72, 79, 132

chakras 22-31
    closing-down 85-87
    color 23, 31, 48-49, 106-107
    emotions 106-109
    endocrine system 47
    healing 70-73, 76-80, 84
    position/function 21, 22-25
    sensing 26-27
children 96-99
circulatory system 38-39
clairvoyance 14, 17, 21, 132
client, meeting 68-69
color
    aura 17
    breathing 43, 50-51, 137
    chakras 23, 31, 48-49, 106-107
consciousness 13, 15, 76, 95, 96, 100
counseling skills 68, 134-135
crown chakra 23, 25, 47, 49, 72, 79

death 110, 112-113, 141
distant healing 114-119
dreams 122-123, 131

emotions 14, 15, 16, 91, 93, 105-109, 137
endocrine system 46-47, 54, 73
energy
    balance 60, 62, 75, 80, 84

breathing in 50-51
chakras 29-30, 70, 73, 84
channels 20-21, 22
clearing 61, 62, 85-87
field 16-19
rebalancing 54, 137
sensing 18-19, 70
soul 16, 132-133
subtle 12, 14, 21-22, 29, 38, 89, 132-133
environment 102, 118, 135
etheric, science of 89, 101
etheric body 14-15, 16, 20-21, 29, 38-39

feet 28-29, 73, 75, 83

group healing 116-117

hands 18, 28
healing
    applications 90-119
    creating channel 121-137
    distant 114-119
    preparation 52-65
    procedure 66-87
    source 7, 28, 61, 67, 69
    triangle 68, 69
heart chakra 23, 24, 28, 49, 72, 79
history 8-11, 16-17, 100-101

illness
    cause 13, 14
    serious/terminal 110-111
intuitive awareness 14, 25, 64-65, 76, 132-133

life force 39, 40, 42
love 7, 13, 14, 24, 28, 63, 94

meditation 128-129
mental energy 16, 136
mental healing 93, 104-105
mental relaxation 58-59

nervous system 44-45
nutrition 124-125

Oneness 12-13, 16-17, 25, 89, 96, 124, 128

plants 102-103
polarity balance 29-30, 50, 70, 73, 75, 76, 80, 83
prayer 126-127
pregnancy 95
protection 87, 136
psychic awareness 14, 17, 20, 21, 25, 132

records 87
relaxation 54-59
religion 9-10, 17, 62, 126-127
respiratory system 40-43
room, preparation 62-63, 85

sacral chakra 23, 24, 47, 49, 50, 73, 79
self
    awareness 130-131, 135
    care for 136-137
    development 122-137
    healing 90-93
shoulders 29, 30, 80, 83
skeleton 36-37, 70, 74-75, 81-83
sleep 55, 57, 122-123, 131
solar disk 137
solar plexus chakra 23, 24, 47, 49, 51, 73, 79, 136
soul
    children 96, 97, 99
    energy 16, 132-133
    illness link 7, 13, 14
    journey 14-15, 20-21, 94, 112
    preparation 61
spirit 10, 89, 112
spiritualism 10-11, 135
stress 54-55

Third Eye 132-133
throat chakra 23, 25, 47, 49, 73, 79
training 11, 67, 68, 142-143

vitality 50-51